Guide To The Moon

Moore, Patrick

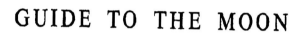

GUIDE TO THE MOON

GUIDE TO THE MOON

by PATRICK MOORE, F.R.A.S.

*Council Member of the British Astronomical Association (Secretary,
Lunar Section), Fellow of the British Interplanetary Society (Council
Member), Member of the Irish Astronomical Society, Member of the
Association of Lunar and Planetary Observers, Corresponding
Member of the Planetensektion der Sternfreunde, etc.*

London
EYRE & SPOTTISWOODE

This book, first published in 1953, is printed in Great
Britain for Eyre & Spottiswoode (Publishers), Ltd.,
15, Bedford Street, London, W.C.2, by Billing and
Sons, Ltd., Guildford and Esher

To F. HADLAND DAVIS

ACKNOWLEDGEMENTS

THIS book may be said to have grown out of a lecture which I delivered to the British Interplanetary Society, in London, in December 1951. I did not, however, know at that time that Dr. H. P Wilkins, who is the Director of the Lunar Section of the British Astronomical Association, author of the 300-inch lunar map, and universally recognized as the leading authority upon the moon, had independently commenced writing a book upon similar lines. It is strange that neither of us should have mentioned it to the other, as we have been very closely associated in lunar work during recent years, and had actually been together at the Meudon Observatory, near Paris, only a few weeks previously.

It is true that independent books produced by Dr. Wilkins and myself would necessarily contain many of the same ideas; and, with generosity which will in no way surprise those who know him, Dr. Wilkins discontinued his own work and made available to me all the material and notes which he had collected for it. I have therefore been able to use these in the present book, and several chapters, notably 1, 3 and 4, are based entirely on them. Dr. Wilkins has continued to give me advice and assistance throughout the compilation of the book, and my debt to him is very great.

There are others, too, who have helped to make the writing of this book easy; and my special thanks are due to A. L. Helm, of the British Interplanetary Society, who has provided some of the plates and drawings, checked the whole manuscript, and made many helpful suggestions, as well as assisting with the proof-reading. His help has been invaluable.

I also owe much to David P. Barcroft, of Madera, California, who has gone to a great deal of trouble to provide me with material which I could not otherwise have obtained, and to John Smith, who read through the original draft and made a number of most helpful comments; while Arthur C. Clarke, Chairman of the British Interplanetary Society and one of the world's leading authorities on the new science of 'astronautics', read through the two chapters dealing with space-flight. Professor W. H. Haas, of Las Cruces, and Dr. E. J. Öpik, of Armagh Observatory, have sent me valuable information about lunar meteors.

The full moon photograph was taken by E. A. Whitaker, and my thanks are due to the Astronomer Royal, who has kindly allowed me to reproduce it. Mr. Whitaker also provided the eclipse list given in the Appendix; and L. F. Ball and R. Myer Baum have made available to me some of their splendid lunar drawings. My grateful thanks are also due to W. A. Dovaston for the lunar photograph reproduced in Plate I.   D. W. G. Arthur was good enough to provide his drawing of the Hyginus Cleft, and I must thank the Council of the British Astronomical Association for allowing me to reproduce it.

Finally, I must not forget to express my thanks to Mrs. Grace Hogarth, who originally suggested that I should write this book, and to the publishers, who have made my task a very pleasant one.

P. M.

CONTENTS

PLATES

FIGURES

11

MAP

FOREWORD

by H. PERCY WILKINS, F.R.A.S., *Director of the Lunar Section of the British Astronomical Association*

THIS guide to the moon will undoubtedly meet a long-felt want, namely that of a really 'popular' book on the nearest of all celestial bodies, the moon.

Without going into minute details, and avoiding mathematics as far as possible, these pages give all the essential facts about the moon in a clear and accurate presentation such as only a diligent student and a practised writer can produce. Mr. Moore possesses both these qualities; he has worked closely with myself in lunar observation, and I have every confidence in his judgement. In addition to the more elementary facts pertaining to our satellite, some of the very latest results, obtained with the aid of some of the finest telescopes in the world, are incorporated, thus increasing the value of the work.

This is the kind of book that should appeal to all lovers of science. Who knows but that this work will introduce the wonders of the heavens to some new Pickering or Barnard or Mädler, who will trace his first interest in astronomy to the book now offered to the English-speaking world by one who has honestly trod the path of observation, so as to have reached a position of authority in the subject?

It has been a pleasure to have been able to afford Mr. Moore some slight assistance with this work, and I fully commend it; it is accurate, factual and informative, while at the same time written in a style that compels the reader to finish the chapters, at once gaining knowledge and with a feeling that the moon has been 'brought down' to him, no longer a strange and mysterious world, but one explained and demonstrated in language that can be understood without effort.

H. P. W.

CHAPTER 1

THE LUNAR WORLD

THOUSANDS upon thousands of years ago, at the dawn of human history, Stone Age men gazed at the moon, and wondered just what it was. It appeared far larger and brighter than any of the stars, or even the five 'wandering stars' that we now call the planets; it moved quickly through the heavens, changing shape regularly from a slender crescent to a full circle, and back again. Surely it must be a god, or at least the dwelling-place of a god?

Moreover, the ancient peoples found the moon very useful. In those dim and far-off times, when lack of alertness meant certain death, dark nights were the most dangerous ones; moonlight gave some defence against surprise attacks by human or animal enemies. Small wonder that the Queen of Night was regarded as truly divine. Knowledge that the moon is a rocky world, smaller than the earth but in some ways comparable to it, came much later; and the new conception of our satellite, as a world which can be reached and colonized, only dates from the last quarter-century.

The ancient races also found that the moon helped them to measure time. The interval from one full moon to the next was found to be more or less constant, and the first rough calendars were drawn up to conform with it. It was also noticed at a very early stage that the ocean tides were regulated by the moon, although it was not known why.

Moon-myths and moon worship

Moon-myths probably go back as far as man himself. Some of the old stories are charming, and seem to be much the same all over the world – which is rather strange, in view of the fact that we have no proofs of any direct contact between the early races of different continents. For instance, who has not heard of the man in the moon? It is true that, by an effort of imagination,

15

the dark patches on the lunar disk can be twisted into something like a human form; but the resemblance between the various myths is very striking. According to a German legend, the Old Man was a villager caught in the act of stealing cabbages, and placed in the moon as a warning to others. Another version, from the island of Sylt, makes him a sheep-stealer, and he is also a thief in a legend from far-off Polynesia, in the South Seas. However, human beings did not monopolize the ancient moon. Hares, cats, toads and frogs also found their way there at various times, each one with its own particular legend.

One more story, this time from China, is perhaps worthy of mention. It is said that there was once a great drought, and a herd of elephants came to drink from a sheet of water called the Moon Lake. They trampled down so many of the local hare population that the next time they appeared, a far-sighted hare pointed out that they were annoying the moon-goddess by disturbing her reflection in the water. The elephants agreed that this was most unwise, and departed hastily.

True moon-worship still persists among the backward tribes of Central Africa, and two thousand years ago the moon was considered one of the most powerful of all the gods. Generally it was male, and second only to the sun in importance. The ancient Egyptians, for instance, had two moon-gods, Khonsu (also the god of time) and Thoth; and as late as the eighth century A.D., the Druids of Britain still paid homage to the moon – we learn this from the Confessional of Ecgbert, Archbishop of York.

What is the moon?

However, the early peoples managed to find out a great deal about the moon itself. At first they believed that it actually changed shape from night to night (in Bushman mythology, the moon was believed to have offended the sun, and was periodically pierced by the solar rays until he pleaded for mercy and was gradually restored!); but it was soon realized that this was not so, as the 'dark' part of the disk could often be seen shining faintly beside the brilliant crescent. We know now that this faint luminosity is due to the earth shining on the moon. The correct explanation was not given until many centuries later, by the

'Forerunner', Leonardo da Vinci; but at least the earthlight showed our ancestors that the moon is always round. Moreover, it was realized that the dark patches on the disk always kept the same positions, proving that the same face was always turned towards us. The nature of these dark patches was, of course, uncertain. Some races believed them to be the reflections of earthly lands and seas, while others attributed them to dense lunar forests.

Then came the Greeks, and with them a complete revision of human thought. Strange though some of their ideas seem today, there can be no doubt that they were the first 'scientists' in the true sense of the word.

Greek astronomy really begins with Thales of Miletus, born in 611 B.C., but for over two centuries the great philosophers held very curious views about the moon. Listen, for instance, to Anaximander, a younger contemporary of Thales: "The moon is a circle nineteen times as large as the earth; it is like a chariot-wheel, the rim of which is hollow and full of fire, as that of the sun also is; it has one vent, like the nozzle of a pair of bellows; its eclipses depend upon the turnings of the wheel". However, the later Greeks knew quite well that the moon does not shine by its own light They discovered that it merely reflects the rays of the sun, so that moonlight is really nothing more than re-flected sunlight. They knew, too, why the moon shows its monthly changes of shape. Democritus, who lived about 450 B.C., believed that there were lofty mountains and hollow valleys on the lunar surface; and gradually the idea that the moon is a rugged, rocky world began to gain popularity. Aristarchus of Samos, who lived about three centuries before Christ, even had a very good idea of the moon's distance from the earth.

But the Greeks, enlightened though they were in many ways, could make no real progress in the physical study of the moon – for the simple reason that they could not see it well enough. The moon is a quarter of a million miles away, and no human eye can make out much detail at such a distance. Short of going there, which has become a workable possibility only during the last few years, the only solution was to bring the moon closer to us. It was the old problem of Mahomet and the mountain, and it was solved, in effect, by the invention of the telescope.

B

The moon through the telescope

Towards the end of the thirteenth century, it was discovered that light is bent or 'refracted' when it passes through curved transparent substances, such as glass. Lenses of this type were used as spectacles for correcting defects in the eye, and in 1608 Hans Lippersheim, a spectacle-maker of Middelburg in Holland, found that by combining various lenses he could obtain an enlarged picture of any distant object. Lippersheim's discovery came to the ears of the great Italian scientist, Galileo, who promptly copied it; and on a memorable evening in the year 1609, the 'telescope' was first turned toward the moon.

Galileo saw at once that the lunar surface was not in the least like that of the earth. Here were no grassy plains, glittering oceans or spreading forests. Instead, he could make out rugged mountains and circular ranges of hills, enclosing sunken amphitheatres, now called 'craters' for want of a better name, while the dark patches forming the figure of the legendary Old Man proved to be lower-lying, more level plains. Truly, the moon was a strange world.

Galileo and his successors spent a great deal of time in lunar study, and a century ago it was popularly supposed that we had found out all about the moon. It was known that it kept the same face permanently towards us because it turned once on its axis in the same time that it took to revolve once round the earth (just over twenty-seven days); that it was 2,160 miles in diameter, so that if it could be dropped into the Atlantic Ocean it would just touch England on one side and North America on the other; and that it lacked air, water, and – so far as could be made out – life. In fact, it was a dead, uninteresting globe, a burnt-out planet of eternal silence where all change had ceased countless æons ago.

Nowadays we have different ideas. We believe, for instance, that the moon is not completely changeless. It is true that there is not much activity on the surface, but here and there we can trace landslips, glows and mists, and it is even within the bounds of possibility that certain very low forms of vegetation still manage to eke out a precarious existence on the inhospitable surface. There may also be a little air left – not nearly enough for us to breathe, but quite enough to form an effective shield against the rocky meteorites which would otherwise bombard the lunar surface from outer space, and make conditions there very uncomfortable.

Voyaging to the moon

Moreover, the moon has assumed a new importance within the last twenty years. We no longer worship it, and we no longer believe it to be the abode of either men or gods; but we do believe that some time within the next century we shall be able to set foot upon it.

The idea of space-travel is far from new. It goes back to the ancient Greeks, and the stories written about it must number millions; but it was bound to remain only a dream while men were still unable to lift themselves more than a few feet above the surface of the earth. It is only within the last 170 years that we have learned to fly; and a century ago, the British jet-fighter or the American Superfortress would have seemed more far-fetched, to ordinary people, than interplanetary travel does now.

Strangely enough, distance is not the main trouble. An aircraft which has made ten circuits of the earth has more than covered the distance to the moon. The real difficulty is the earth's gravitational pull. All bodies possess gravity, and the more massive the body the stronger the pull; the earth is very massive indeed, and unless we go on applying power all the time, which would be hopelessly uneconomical, we cannot escape without working up to a speed of seven miles a second. Balloons and aeroplanes, of course, are useless. Both depend upon air for their lift, and out in space there is no air. The atmospheric blanket surrounding our world is very shallow, and no aeroplane can rise more than a few miles. Fortunately, however, lack of air does not affect the performance of a rocket, and it is in the rocket motor that our main hopes are centred.

The moon is the obvious target for our first space-voyage, partly because we know so much about conditions there and partly because it is so close. Venus, nearest of the planets, is a hundred times as far off, and a journey there will take months instead of days. Moreover, the experience gained on the earth-moon trip will enable us to find out whether it is possible to attempt longer voyages. On the whole, we have no reason to believe that we shall encounter any difficulties which cannot be overcome.

As to the moon itself? Perhaps it does not seem an inviting world; but well as the surface has been mapped, there are many wonders in store for the first explorers. Our earth has been ransacked. Modern man sighs for 'new worlds to conquer', and the solar system awaits his inspection. He has the ability, and he is gaining the knowledge; and provided that he keeps his senses, he stands on the threshold of the space age.

*

CHAPTER 2

A PICTURE OF THE UNIVERSE

THE moon is such a splendid object in our sky that we naturally tend to regard it as a most important astronomical body. Actually, however, it is very insignificant. It appears large and bright only because it is so close, and in any case we have learned that even our own earth is tiny indeed.

Before we can really form a proper idea of the moon's position in the universe, we must have some knowledge of the larger scheme of things. Our immediate neighbours, even the sun itself, are mere specks in the cosmos—single grains of sand upon a seashore. What lies beyond them, in the boundless void?

The solar system

The solar system, our home, is made up of one star (the sun), nine major planets, thirty moons or 'satellites', thousands of small planets or 'asteroids', and a large number of comets and meteor swarms. On the whole it is a compact family, and the sun rules it with an iron hand.

The human brain is not capable of appreciating vast distances. We may talk of 'a million miles', but we cannot really understand what is meant. Instead of using actual figures, then, let us imagine that the sun has been reduced to a globe 2 feet in diameter. Using this as a basis, we can fill in the rest of the solar system to scale.

The first of the nine planets, Mercury, will be represented by a grain of mustard seed, circling the central globe at a distance of 164 feet. Venus will become a pea at a distance of 284 feet; the earth, another pea, at 430 feet; and Mars, outermost of the 'interior' group of planets, a pin's head at 654 feet. Before going any further, let us put in the satellites. Mercury and Venus have none; the moon will become another grain of mustard seed,

circling the earth at a distance of 13 inches; and Phobos and
Deimos, the two tiny attendants of Mars, will be so small that
we shall have to use a powerful microscope to see them at all.

All four interior planets are solid and rocky, and have some
points in common. Mercury, not much larger than the moon,
is an uncomfortable world with only a trace of air; Venus, the
lovely 'evening star', is a planet of mystery, as our telescopes
cannot see through her dense, cloudy atmosphere. Mars, the red
planet, is often considered to be the one other world where
higher forms of life could exist, but conditions do not appear
to be very favourable there. The atmosphere is very thin; there
is little water, and most of the surface is desert.

Outside Mars we meet the asteroids, about 1,000 feet from
our 2-foot sun and represented by grains of sand. Most of these
Lilliputian worlds are mere lumps of rock, and it is possible that
they are the shattered fragments of an old planet which somehow came to grief

Beyond the asteroid belt come the four giants of the solar
system – Jupiter, an orange, half a mile from the central globe;
Saturn, a tangerine at four-fifths of a mile; Uranus, a plum at
rather more than a mile; and Neptune, another plum, at two
and a half miles. All these planets seem to be at a comparatively
early stage of evolution, which is natural enough when we remember that they are far larger than the earth, and have cooled
down less rapidly. Jupiter is thought to have a rocky core, surrounded by a thick layer of ice which is in turn overlaid by a
deep, gaseous atmosphere made up mainly of evil-smelling
hydrogen compounds such as ammonia and methane; and the
other giants are probably built on much the same pattern. Of
more interest to us at present are their moons. Jupiter has
twelve, four of which are of considerable size and the rest
minute. The two largest members of the Jovian family, Gany-
mede and Callisto, are actually larger than the planet Mercury,
so that on our scale they will become small pins'-heads. Titan,
the chief of Saturn's nine satellites, is not much smaller than
Mars, and has even been found to possess an atmosphere—
though this atmosphere seems to be composed mainly of
methane (the pungent gas known to miners as the dreaded 'fire-
damp') and is certainly unbreathable. Uranus has five satellites,

all rather small, and Neptune two, one of which is the size of Mercury and the other very tiny.

Finally, far out in the wastes, we meet with barren, frozen, dimly-lit little Pluto, most recently discovered of the sun's family – another pin's-head on our scale, with a curiously elliptical orbit which sometimes carries it more than three miles from our central globe. There are some strange problems connected with Pluto, and some authorities consider that it *is* nothing more than a former satellite of Neptune which somehow managed to break away from the pull of its parent.

Comets and meteors may be regarded as the 'stray' members of the solar system. A comet is not a solid body like a planet. It is made up of rocky particles enveloped in a cloud of gas, and is so flimsy and unsubstantial that if it is incautious enough to pass close to a major planet it is liable to have its orbit violently twisted – it may even be hurled clean out of the solar system. Meteors are small pieces of rock, travelling round the sun in swarms. If a meteor comes close enough to the earth to be drawn down by the terrestrial gravitational pull, it burns away by friction against the particles of the upper atmosphere, giving rise to the appearance known as a 'shooting-star'. One or two fairly bright shooting-stars can be seen on any night of the year, and fainter ones are very common; but on the rare occasions when the earth ploughs through a dense shoal – as happened in 1833 and 1866 – a splendid display results. Unusually large meteors may manage to reach the earth's surface before being burned away, and one, found by Peary in Greenland, weighed as much as 36 tons.

Beyond the solar system

So much for the sun's family. It seems very important to us, but once again we are deceiving ourselves. All the bodies of the solar system are comparatively closely packed, and beyond Pluto comes a vast stretch of empty space – the absolute isolation of our planetary system is something we find very hard to appreciate. Let us go back to our scale model for a moment. If we put our 2-foot sun inside the Tower of London, Pluto will be somewhere near the Houses of Parliament; but what about the nearest star? We shall not find it in England, or even in Europe. It will lie 8,000 miles away, in the frozen wastes of Siberia; and all but the half-dozen nearest stars will have to be placed clear of the earth altogether.

We had better abandon our scale model, and look for a new unit of distance. Fortunately, there is a convenient one. As long ago as 1676, a Danish astronomer, Olaus Römer, discovered that light does not travel instantaneously; it moves at 186,000 miles a second, so that it would leap from the earth to the moon in a second and a half. The 93-million-mile journey to the sun would take eight minutes, and to reach Pluto would require six hours; but the nearest star could not be reached in less than four years! The distance covered by a light-ray in one year (the 'light-year') is just under 6 million million miles, and this unit is often used for measuring the distances of bodies outside our own system.

A star is a sun – or, to put it more forcibly, our own blinding sun turns out to be nothing more than a normal star, far less splendid than many of those we can see any night of the year. It would need 20,000 suns to match the brilliancy of Rigel, the bluish star at the foot of Orion; but Rigel is over 500 light-years away, so that the rays now entering our eyes started on their journey when Henry VI was king of England, and the Wars of the Roses had only just begun. However, there are many much less luminous stars. If we represent the sun by an ordinary electric light bulb, the most luminous stars will be powerful searchlights – the feeblest, tiny glow-worms.

All the stars are moving at high speeds, but at their immense distances they appear to all intents and purposes fixed in their positions on the celestial vault. Their individual movements can be detected, but only with delicate instruments over periods of months, and the constellations described by the great Greek astronomer, Ptolemy, 2,000 years ago, are almost the same as those we see now. Only the moon and the planets, or 'wandering stars' as they were once called, are close enough to show obvious changes in position from night to night.

Our own system of stars, known as the 'Milky Way' or Galaxy, is shaped like a vast cartwheel, and is about 100,000 light-years in diameter. It is not, however, the only one. Far away in space, so remote that their light takes millions of years to reach us, lie other galaxies; if space was perfectly transparent (which is not the case–the emptiest regions still contain a certain amount of matter), it has been estimated that 100 million of them could be photographed with our most powerful telescopes. Bearing in mind that we can only see one tiny corner of the universe, we realize that our own solar system is insignificant indeed, with the moon one of the junior members of it. Moreover there are certainly many other solar systems, comparable to ours, among the countless stars of the galaxies.

One final word must be said about the scale of the universe. A lunar voyage would take less than a week, and even Pluto could be reached in a reasonable time; but the stars are almost inconceivably remote, and even if we could move at the speed of light–which we shall never be able to do–it would take many years to travel to them. Interplanetary flight is more than a possibility; it is almost with us. Interstellar flight, on the other hand, is likely to remain nothing more than a fantastic dream.

The suns and galaxies of outer space have a fascination of their own; but we know that they are for ever beyond our reach, and it is a relief to turn back from these remote regions to our nearby, familiar moon.

CHAPTER 3

THE BIRTH OF THE MOON

AT the present time, we have to admit that the origin of the earth itself remains something of a mystery. Many theories have been put forward, but each one has its drawbacks, and the whole question remains very open. It seems certain that the earth was formed either from the sun, a second star associated with the sun, or a cloud of rarefied gas surrounding the sun; and it was probably born between two and three thousand million years ago. Apart from this, we know nothing really definite about the past history of the solar system.

Obviously, then, we cannot be at all positive as to how the moon came into being; but we can at least make some intelligent guesses, in the hope of stumbling upon at least part of the truth.

There can be no doubt that the moon was once hot. Like the earth and all other large solid bodies in the solar system, it is more or less spherical; and unless it had once been in a molten condition, it could not possibly have taken on such a form. By now, however, it has lost most of its internal heat. The earth has solidified to a great extent, but the moon has cooled down even more, for the simple reason that it is smaller. A large mass will always keep its heat longer than a small one, and therefore the fact that the moon has lost more of its heat than the earth is no indication that it is older.

In 1796 Laplace, a famous French mathematician, put forward a theory of the origin of the solar system which was universally accepted for many years. According to him, the sun was once surrounded by a vast cloud of tenuous gas, which contracted and split up into rings, each ring finally condensing into a gaseous planet. The earth, one of these newly formed bodies, contracted towards its own centre of gravity and threw off a ring of its own, which condensed into the moon.

Unfortunately, Laplace's 'nebular hypothesis' has not stood the test of time. Mathematical arguments have shown that the matter left behind as the gas-cloud shrank would not form definite rings, and in any case material in rings of such a kind could never condense into definite masses. The theory has, therefore, been abandoned.

The tidal theory

In the latter part of the nineteenth century, an English mathematician, G. H. Darwin (son of Charles Darwin, the great naturalist), worked out the possible history of the earth-moon system, starting from the assumption that the two bodies were originally one. He concluded that the moon was thrown off not as a gaseous ring, but as a compact fluid mass. According to the modern version of this theory, the earth had cooled sufficiently to possess a thin crust before the separation took place. The earth, rotating rapidly upon its axis, was in the state known as 'unstable equilibrium', so that it became elliptical in form, rotating about its shorter axis. Two main forces were acting upon it – the tides raised upon it by the sun, and its own natural period of vibration. When these two forces were 'in resonance', i.e. acted together, the tides increased to such an extent that the whole body became first pear-shaped and then dumb-bell-shaped, with one 'bell' (the earth) much larger than the other (the future moon). Eventually the neck of the dumb-bell broke altogether, and a new world had been born.

Professor W. H. Pickering, a well-known American lunar observer, went further, and pointed out that if this theory was correct the thin crust of the otherwise fluid earth must have been torn apart, leaving a huge hollow where the thrown-off mass had lain. Moreover, the shock caused by the final fracture would have been violent enough to crack the crust in other places.

A glance at a terrestrial map or globe shows clearly that if the opposite sides of the Atlantic Ocean could be clapped together, they would fit almost perfectly. Allowing for the sea having washed away portions of the land here and there, and supposing Britain and France to be joined – as was the case in prehistoric times, when the Channel and the North Sea formed a low-lying land instead of a shallow sea – the relationship is obvious. The 'bulge' of Africa fits into the hollow of South America, and the eastern coast of North America corresponds to the western coast of Europe. The Pacific Ocean, on the other hand, is almost circular, and so vast that to an observer on Venus or Mars it would appear as a patch occupying sometimes nearly the whole of the earth's visible disk. Pickering's suggestion was that the great, rounded hollow which now forms the bed of the Pacific is nothing more nor less than the scar left in the earth's crust by the breaking-off of the moon, so that our satellite was born at the spot where our greatest ocean now rolls.

The crust of the earth cracked under the shock, and portions of it floated apart, to settle down eventually in the places where we now find Eurasia and the Americas. They did not, of course, float in water; all the water now in the oceans was then suspended in the dense, steamy atmosphere. The crustal cracking exposed the fiery interior of the earth, and the fragments of the crust floated as skin or scum on the hot, molten globe. The lava surface exposed between the broken pieces of the crust eventually cooled and solidified, and later, when water was able to settle on the surface, became the Atlantic Ocean.

Other theories

This picture of the earth as a globe of fiery lava, covered with a hot, thin crust and finally hurling off the moon, is a fascinating one, but we have no proof that it is correct. Most leading authorities now consider that the moon is not a proper 'satellite' at all, but a true planet, either born close to the earth or subsequently captured by our powerful gravitational pull. Support for this theory is given by the fact that the moon appears to be disturbingly large for a mere satellite. It is not the largest satellite in the solar system, but it is much the largest in relation to its primary, as is shown in Fig. 1. The moon has $\frac{1}{4}$ of the diameter of the earth and $\frac{1}{81}$ of its mass; Titan, the largest of Saturn's nine satellites, has only $\frac{1}{20}$ the diameter and $\frac{1}{4700}$ the mass of Saturn—despite the fact that Titan is considerably bigger than the moon. Therefore, it seems best to treat the earth-moon system as a double planet rather than as a planet and a satellite.

According to a theory recently put forward by Von Weizsäcker, which has gained considerable support, the earth and moon were never one. The planets are supposed to have been formed after the sun had ploughed through a comparatively dense interstellar cloud, collecting a gaseous envelope which eventually condensed into planets. The inner satellites of the great planets (Jupiter, Saturn, Uranus and Neptune) were formed inside the atmospheres of their parents, but the other

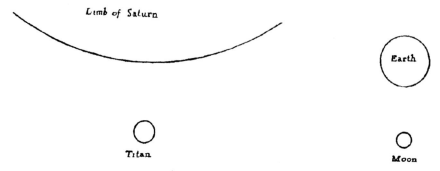

Fig. 1. SIZES OF TITAN AND THE MOON COMPARED TO THEIR PRIMARIES

(All four are drawn to the same scale)

moons of the solar system, including our own, were separate condensation products, captured by the major planets at a later stage.

At the moment, we cannot definitely decide between the rival theories. Each has its strong points, each has its weaknesses; and there is no chance of solving the problem until we have cleared up the mystery of how the solar system itself came into being.

Effects of the tides

At any rate, there is no possible doubt that at an earlier stage of evolution, the moon was much closer to the earth than it is to-day. In those far-off times, the 'month', the time taken for the moon to revolve once round the earth, was of course much shorter than it is now. At a distance of 11,000 miles, the moon would make a complete circuit in only six and a half hours, and the earth's 'day' was then about the same length, six and a half hours. It is clear that the tides raised by the two globes on each other must have been extremely violent. Even at its present distance of a quarter of a million miles, the moon causes high oceanic tides; at a mere 11,000 miles, these tides must have been truly Titanic. But the massive earth pulls much more strongly than the moon, so that the moon was the greater sufferer. These mutual tides had two important results. They slowed down the axial rotations of both earth and moon, and they pushed the moon further away.

As the torn, tide-rent moon receded, a solid crust formed over its surface. The persistent terrestrial pull raised a permanent 'bulge', or semi-solid tidal wave, on the lunar globe, and did its best to keep the bulge turned towards the earth. Obviously this acted as a brake, and the moon's axial spin was slowed down still more. The earth's 'day' was lengthened, too, by the lunar tides; and these processes continued for millions of years, until the moon's rate of spin had been so greatly reduced that, relatively to the earth (though not, of course, to the sun) it had ceased to rotate at all. One face of the moon was turned permanently earthward, the other away; and the 'month' had become 27·3 of our modern days. Meanwhile, the earth's period of axial rotation had increased to twenty-four hours.

The mere fact that the moon now keeps the same hemisphere permanently towards us is positive proof that the two bodies were once close together, as there can be no doubt that the earth's gravitational pull is responsible for this state of affairs. Moreover if the moon had been solid from birth, the earth's attraction would not have raised a bulge on the lunar surface, and would have had nothing to grip on in order to slow down the moon's rotation–since the drag on one part of the surface would have been the same as that on another. The moon must then have been plastic. It is significant that the present-day moon is not a perfect sphere, but egg-shaped, with a pronounced bulge towards the centre of the earthward side.

The earth slowed down the moon's rate of spin by pulling on this tidal bulge and using it as a brake. Now that the moon has been forced into a condition in which this bulge is stationary with respect to the earth, the effect has, of course, ceased; but, strangely enough, the moon still manages to cause a slow but sure slowing-down of the earth's rotation. There is no bulge to pull on, as the moon was not massive enough to produce one, but there is something almost as effective – the ocean.

Anyone who has stood on a beach and watched the tide coming in must have realized that a tremendous amount of energy is being used up, particularly in view of the friction of the water against the sea-bed. This energy must come from somewhere, and can only be drawn from the earth itself, which may be likened to a sort of gigantic flywheel. If the tides take up some of the energy which the earth possesses by virtue of its axial spin, the rate of spin must slacken; and this is what is happening. Another result is that the moon is being driven slowly outwards.

The fate of the moon

If we consider one body revolving round another, and multiply together its mass, its distance and its speed, we shall obtain what is called its 'angular momentum'. Both earth and moon revolve round the centre of gravity of the earth-moon system (a fact which is explained more fully in Chapter 4), and each has its own angular momentum. As the moon pulls on the waters of the ocean, the earth slows down and loses some of its angular momentum. But angular momentum can never be destroyed—it can only be transferred, and in this case it is transferred to the moon. In order to increase its own angular momentum, the moon must increase its distance from the earth, and this is what it is actually doing; so that not only is the length of our 'day' increasing, but the moon is slowly spiralling outwards.

Both these effects are inconceivably small. The increase in the length of the day amounts to something like a second in 100,000 years.[1] However, in the far-off times when the coal deposits were being laid down, and huge reptiles were lords of the earth, the days were appreciably shorter than at present.

What of the future? As time goes on the days will become longer and longer, until at last the 'day' and the 'month' will again be equal, each as long as forty-seven of our modern days, so that an ordinary 'morning' will be almost as long as a present fortnight. The moon will then be about 340,000 miles away,

[1] Recent investigations, carried out mainly by H Finch at Greenwich, have shown that the earth is not nearly so good a timekeeper as our modern quartz clocks. The 'day' lengthens and shortens by small amounts for no apparent reason (internal disturbances in the earth itself are probably responsible), but in the long run these irregularities tend to cancel out.

instead of its present 238,000. However, there is no urgent hurry to map the moon before it recedes into the distance. This state of affairs will not arise until about the year A.D. 50,000,000,000!

All lunar tides will then cease. Solar tides, however, will still be acting; and these will gradually slow the earth down still further, while the moon will close in again. In the very distant future, so long ahead that no man can begin to imagine it, the moon will approach so closely that a strange fate will overtake it–it will be broken up into fragments.

The earth's gravitational pull is extremely powerful, as we know, and any solid body coming within a certain safety-limit (known as the 'Roche' limit) would be first stretched, and then shattered. It is possible that the famous rings of Saturn were formed in this way; it is significant that they lie inside the Roche limit for Saturn, whereas all known planetary satellites lie outside the danger-zones of their primaries. If men still live on the earth at that remote epoch, which seems highly doubtful, they will certainly be able to boast of owning a ringed planet; but they will have to do without the moon's friendly light.

CHAPTER 4

THE MOVEMENTS OF THE MOON

THE ancient peoples believed that the sun, moon and stars revolved round the earth, and not until the third century B C. did anyone seriously suggest that this might not be the case. The first to maintain that the earth turned round the sun was a Greek astronomer, Aristarchus of Samos, but the idea did not meet with a favourable reception–indeed, Aristarchus was accused of impiety, brought to trial, and narrowly escaped with his life.

Ptolemy, greatest of the old Greek scientists, went back to the idea of a central earth; and for fifteen centuries the 'Ptolemaic system', according to which all the heavenly bodies revolved round our own world, was universally accepted. Nowadays, we know better. The earth has been relegated to its true status of a very junior member of the sun's family, and even the statement that "the moon revolves round the earth" needs a certain amount of qualification.

Phases of the moon

However, our first task must be to describe the 'phases' of the moon, and for this it will be best to simplify matters as much as possible For the moment, then, let us imagine that the moon revolves round the earth in a perfect circle, going round once every 29½ days. This is shown in Fig. 2, which, like those following, is not to scale.

The moon has no light of its own. It shines only by reflected sunlight, and obviously the sun can only illuminate half of the moon at any one time. In the diagram, the unlighted–and therefore non-luminous–'night' hemisphere is blackened, while the shining or 'day' hemisphere is left white; E represents the earth, S the sun, and M1, M2, M3 and M4 the moon in various positions in its orbit.

Look first at M1. At this moment the earth, moon and sun are more or less in a straight line, with the moon in the middle.

The lighted half is turned towards the sun, and the dark half towards the earth; since the dark half does not shine, the moon cannot be seen at all, and is astronomically 'new'.[1]

From M1, the moon moves in its orbit towards position M2. Gradually, a little of the day hemisphere begins to turn towards the earth, and the familiar crescent makes its appearance in the evening sky; very often the 'night side' can be faintly seen as well, not because the sun is shining on it, but because the earth is. Earthlight on the moon is far more powerful than moonlight on the earth (partly because the earth is much larger, but also because it is a better reflector), and the glare is enough to make

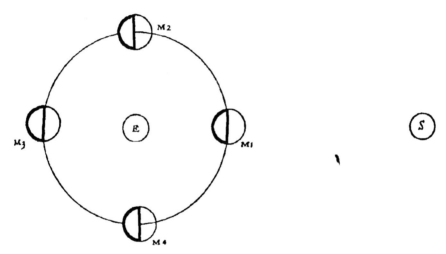

Fig. 2. Phases of the Moon

the night hemisphere dimly luminous. This effect is masked as more and more of the sunlit side appears; by the time M2 is reached, half of the day hemisphere is visible, and the moon is at 'first quarter'.

This term is liable to cause a certain amount of confusion. At 'first quarter', the moon appears as a half. It is logical enough really, however, as the moon has then completed one quarter of its orbit reckoning from new moon to new moon.

From M2 the moon moves steadily on towards M3, and more and more of the day hemisphere comes into view. At this stage

[1] People often speak of the crescent moon as 'new', but this is wrong. The true 'new moon' is totally invisible.

the moon is said to be 'gibbous', i.e. between half and full. By the time M3 is reached, the night hemisphere is turned wholly away from the earth; the lighted half is fully presented, and the moon is full. Once again the earth, moon and sun are more or less in a straight line, but this time the earth is in the middle.

As the moon moves on towards M4, the day hemisphere starts to turn away from us again. Passing through the gibbous stage, the moon has become half again by the time it reaches M4–the phase known as 'last quarter'–and again approaches the sun's line-of-sight, becoming a narrowing crescent and finally disappearing into the morning twilight. After 29½ days it has arrived back at M1, and is again 'new'.

The lunation

A discrepancy may be noticed here. The moon takes only 27⅓ days to circle the earth once; and if we measure its position

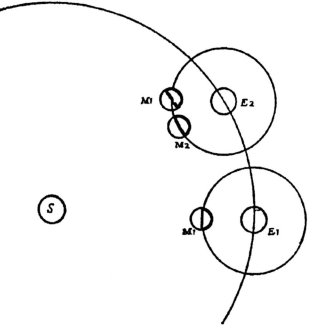

Fig. 3. THE LUNATION

with respect to any particular star (not a planet, of course, because a planet has movement of its own), it will return to the same position in the sky 27⅓ days later. Why, then, is the

interval between new moon and new moon over two days
longer?

The explanation is to be found in the fact that the earth itself
is moving round the sun. Fig. 3 will make the position clear.
Once again S represents the sun, E1 and E2 the earth in different
positions, and M the moon. When the earth is at E1 and the
moon at M1, the moon is, of course, new. $27\frac{1}{3}$ days later the
moon has completed one full circuit, and has arrived back at
M1; but meanwhile the earth has moved on to E2, and the moon
must move some way on–to M2–before the three bodies are
properly lined up again. The extra journey between M1 and M2
takes the moon just over 2 days, which accounts for the difference.

There are technical terms for each of these two periods. The
$27\frac{1}{3}$-day period is known as the moon's 'sidereal period', and
the interval between two successive new moons as the 'lunation',
or 'synodic month'.

The shape of the moon's orbit

The next correction to our simplified picture has to do with
the shape of the moon's path. Ptolemy was more or less correct
in saying that the moon turned round the earth, but his suggested orbit was wildly in error. The ancient astronomers believed that the circle was a perfect form, and that all celestial
bodies must therefore move in circles; but this led to difficulties
in the case of the moon, since the lunar disk sometimes appeared
larger than at others, which showed that its distance from the
earth varied to some extent. It was therefore supposed that
although the moon's orbit was circular, the earth was not
exactly in the centre of the circle; and as further errors arose,
Ptolemy was forced to make his moon move not actually along
the main circle, but in a small circle or 'epicycle', the centre of
which itself moved in a circle. The whole theory was unwieldy
and far-fetched, and more and more epicycles were introduced
as more and more discrepancies appeared, until the system
became hopelessly complicated.

The essence of true science is simplicity. A straightforward
theory is far more likely to be correct than a complex one; and
after the lapse of well over a thousand years, a simple explanation was found.

Nicolaus Copernicus, a Polish canon, was the first to revive Aristarchus' old theory of a sun-centred system, and it was his book, published in 1546, which finally led to the rejection of Ptolemy's ideas. It must be admitted that Copernicus retained many of Ptolemy's mistakes – for instance, he still believed that all celestial orbits were circular, and was even reduced to bringing back epicycles – but he paved the way for Johannes Kepler, who developed the theory and discovered the three famous Laws of Planetary Motion which bear his name. The first of these laws, announced in 1609 (the year in which Galileo made the first telescopic lunar observations), stated that the planets moved around the sun in orbits which were not circular, but elliptical, the sun occupying one focus of the ellipse; and clearly the same held good for the moon – it moved in an elliptical path, with the earth in one of the foci.[1]

The fact that the lunar orbit is not circular means, of course, that the moon is sometimes closer to us than at others, and this accounts for the variations in apparent size. At its closest, or 'perigee', the distance is 226,000 miles; at its farthest, or 'apogee', the moon recedes to 252,000 miles, giving an average of 238,000 – just under a quarter of a million. It will be seen that the variations in distance are quite considerable, and the moon's apparent diameter at apogee is only nine-tenths of what it is at perigee.

The earth-moon system

There is no doubt that the earth-moon system is better regarded as a double planet than as a planet and a satellite. Therefore, it is not entirely correct to say that the moon is revolving round the earth. More properly, both bodies are moving round their common centre of gravity.

To understand this more clearly, let us picture an ordinary gymnasium dumb-bell. Balance it on a post by the joining arm, and twist it; both bells will revolve round the 'centre of gravity'

[1] The best way to draw an ellipse is to stick two pins in a board, an inch or two apart, and fasten them to the ends of a length of cotton, leaving a certain amount of slack. Then draw the cotton tight with the point of a pencil, and trace a curve, keeping the cotton tight all the time. The result will be an oval or ellipse, and the pins will mark the two foci.

of the system, i.e. the point where the arm is supported. Ordinarily this point will be in the middle of the arm, since the bells are of equal weight. If one bell is heavier than the other, the supporting point will have to be moved towards the heavier bell; the greater the difference in weight between the bells, the greater will be the distance of the supporting point from the middle of the arm.

The same holds good for the earth and moon, which may be compared to the two bells. There is no joining arm, but the force of gravitation acts in much the same way. The earth has eighty-one times the mass of the moon, and so the centre of gravity is shifted well towards the earth–so far, in fact, that it actually lies inside the terrestrial globe, though some way from the centre of the earth. It is around this point, the 'barycentre', that the two globes are revolving.[1]

The pull of the sun

Even now there is a further correction to be introduced into our original diagram, which showed the moon going round the earth in a straightforward circular orbit. This arises from the fact that, curious though it may seem, the sun's pull upon the moon is more than twice as powerful as the earth's. To an observer on the sun, the moon would appear as a perfectly normal planet, turning in an elliptical orbit with the sun occupying one of the foci; and in fact it is true to say that the moon revolves round the sun–even though, at the same time, earth and moon are both revolving round their common centre of gravity.

Although the sun's pull is so strong, there is no danger of the moon parting company with the earth and moving off in an orbit entirely its own. This is because the sun pulls the earth and moon almost equally. The moon is the more strongly attracted when it is closer to the sun than the earth is, and less strongly when it is farther away; but the force on the two bodies is always much the same, and all that the earth has to do is to overcome the slight difference. This it can easily manage, and so earth and moon keep together as they travel around the sun.

---

[1] Needless to say, this explanation is very much over-simplified, but the main principle is clear enough.

Eclipses

Although the sun is so much larger than the moon, it is also so much more distant that it appears to us almost exactly the same size. Consequently when earth, sun and moon move into a straight line, with the moon in the middle, the lunar disk blots out the sun, and we witness a solar eclipse. If the moon's orbit was really as simple as it has been drawn in Fig. 2, we should have a solar eclipse at each new moon; but this is not the case, as the moon's orbit is tilted or 'inclined' at an angle of about five degrees, relative to the earth's.

The apparent yearly path of the sun among the stars is known as the ecliptic. It can be worked out very accurately, even though the stars themselves are overpowered while the sun is

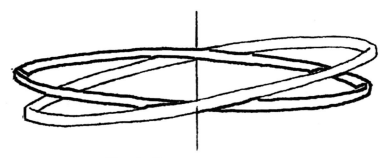

Fig. 4. Two inclined hoops

above the horizon. The monthly path of the moon can of course be plotted, and it is at once clear that it is tilted relative to the ecliptic. The best way of picturing this is to compare the paths to two hoops, hinged along a diameter and at an angle to each other (Fig. 4). The tilted hoop will lie half above and half below its companion, and this is the case with the path of the moon compared to the ecliptic. The two points where the 'hoops' cross are known as the nodes.

We can now see why eclipses are comparatively rare. Unless new moon occurs exactly at a node, no solar eclipse can occur; and the two do not often coincide.

The moon's orbit is not quite the same each revolution. The earth and sun approach and recede, so that their pulls on the moon vary; and in addition, measurable effects are produced

by other planets, particularly Venus.[1] The result of all this is
that the two nodal points appear to move slowly round the sky,
completing the full circuit in just over eighteen years.

The hidden side of the moon

It was realized in very early times that the moon always keeps
the same hemisphere turned towards the earth. A marking
which lies near the centre of the lunar disk will always stay
there; it will not drift about This is in marked contrast to
Mars, for instance, whose markings can be seen moving steadily
across the disk from east to west as the Red Planet spins on its
axis.[2] However, it is possible for us to peer a little way round
alternate edges of the moon, owing to what is known as 'libration'.

Because the moon's distance from the earth varies, it does not
maintain a constant speed in its orbit. When it is distant, it
moves more slowly; when it closes in, its speed increases. But
the rate of axial spin does not alter. Consequently, the orbital
speed is sometimes too fast to keep pace with the steady axial
rotation, sometimes too slow; and the result is that instead of
the moon always keeping exactly the same face towards us, it
seems to sway a little. We can thus see some way round first
the eastern and then the western edge, obtaining very foreshortened views of the normally hidden hemisphere. This effect
is known as the 'libration in longitude'.

Moreover, it is clear that as the moon is sometimes north and
sometimes south of the position it would occupy if its orbit was
not tilted, we can also see some way beyond alternate poles.
This is the 'libration in latitude'.

The sum total of all this is that instead of seeing only half
the lunar surface, we can actually examine four-sevenths. The
remaining three-sevenths is permanently turned away from us,
and though we have a reasonably good idea of what it must be
like (see Chapter 12), it will remain uncharted until the first

---

[1] It is often thought that Mars is the nearest of the planets, but this is an error.
Mars can never approach nearer than 35 million miles, whereas Venus may come
within 24 million Moreover, Venus is considerably more massive than Mars, so
that its gravitational pull is more powerful
[2] The Martian 'day' is only about half an hour longer than our own

space-ships land on the moon, or a rocket-carried camera circles the lunar globe.

Secular acceleration

One further peculiarity of the lunar movement should perhaps be mentioned: the moon appears to be speeding up in its orbit Of course, the velocity near perigee is appreciably greater than that near apogee, but if we take the position of the moon as determined centuries ago, and predict the present position by adding on the correct number of revolutions, a discrepancy will be found; the moon will have moved too far, i.e. too quickly.

Fortunately the ancient astronomers could leave us reliable records, as they observed eclipses. A total eclipse of the sun can only happen at new moon; therefore, the moment of totality is also the exact moment of new moon, and eclipse records go back for thousands of years. It was by comparing these observations with modern measures of the moon's position that the speeding-up, or 'secular acceleration', was discovered. It is partly caused by Venus and Mars pulling on the earth, making our path round the sun less elliptical (though even now it does not depart much from a circle), and partly by the tidal effects described in the last chapter. The effect is very small, but over hundreds of years it mounts up sufficiently to be measured with some accuracy.

Clearly, then, the moon's movements are by no means so simple as they appear at first sight. To explain them completely taxes even our greatest mathematicians; but it is now time for us to turn to the lunar world itself.

CHAPTER 5

OBSERVERS OF THE MOON

EVEN a small telescope will show that the moon is very different from the earth. In place of our own prairies, forests, lakes and ice-fields, we find a rocky, rugged surface–barren, waterless and almost airless, with none of the soft half-tones we are used to. The moon is a world of harsh lights and uncompromising black-and-white. Here, perhaps more than anywhere else in the solar system, we see Nature's original work unaltered by the passing of time.

Towering mountains rise from the plains, mingling with ridges, hillocks, valleys and deep yawning cracks; here and there, a bright starlike peak glitters against the dark background, and curious whitish streaks, known as 'rays', run for immense distances across the surface. But the most striking features of all are the craters. There are hundreds upon hundreds of them, scattered all over the moon, ranging from tremendous walled enclosures large enough to contain a dozen English counties or a whole American state down to tiny pits, so small that they are at the limit of visibility. Some have smooth interiors; some contain lofty central mountains, some have been broken and ruined by others, so that only disjoined parts of their original walls now remain.

The earliest telescopes

Galileo's original telescope, though it only magnified thirty times, was quite powerful enough to show him many of the features of the lunar landscape, and modern astronomy really begins on that epoch-making moment in 1609 when he first turned his newly-made 'optick tube' to the heavens. Fittingly enough, the moon was the first thing he looked at, and during the next few years he even constructed a chart of the principal features–crude and inaccurate, needless to say, but marking the beginning of true 'selenography',[1] or lunar study.

[1] A word derived from the Greek· Selene, the moon-goddess

Galileo also tried to measure the heights of some of the lunar peaks. His method was not capable of any great accuracy, and his results were somewhat wide of the mark; but he concluded that some of the mountains reached altitudes of about 5¼ miles, which is at least in the right order of magnitude.

While Galileo was observing the moon from Italy, news of the new invention spread. During 1610 telescopes, or 'perspective cylinders' as they were then called, were brought to England. Strangely enough the first British lunar observations do not come from London, Bath or York, but from the isolated country village in Pembrokeshire–Traventy–where Sir William Lower used one of the 'cylinders' to view the moon. Lower described the broad plains, ring-mountains and other features just as Galileo had done, and said that about half-moon he could see "the mountain-tops shining like stars", while the full moon resembled a tart his cook had made–"there a bit of bright stuff, there some dark, and so confused all over".

Lower and Galileo agreed on one important point: there were no half-lights on the moon. Objects were either brilliantly lit, or immersed in absolute blackness. There was, in fact, no twilight. We know now that this is because of the almost complete absence of air, though the fact that the moon has no appreciable atmospheric covering was not fully realized until many years after Galileo and Lower had made their first observations.

One of the obvious features of the lunar face was its division into bright upland areas, and dark, lower-lying plains. The latter were christened 'seas', and are still called by romantic names such as the Sea of Serenity (in Latin, Mare Serenitatis) and the Sea of Nectar (Mare Nectaris). Galileo himself seems to have been well aware that there was no water in them, but most astronomers of the time (including Kepler, the great mathematician who discovered the Laws of Planetary Motion) thought differently, and it was generally believed that the moon was a smaller edition of the earth, with lakes, oceans and–presumably–inhabitants. Of course, it was impossible to find out much with the first telescopes. The moon is a quarter of a million miles away, and Galileo, using a magnifying power of thirty, was able to see it about as well as he could have done with the naked eye at a distance of 8,000 miles. No wonder that small details escaped him.

Hevelius and Riccioli

During the next thirty years, several charts were made by various observers, but none of these were of any real value, and the first reasonably accurate map was produced in 1647 by Hevelius, a city councillor of Danzig. Hevelius built an observatory on the roof of his house, and equipped it with the best instruments available at the time, he was moreover a patient and skilful observer, and his map, just under a foot in diameter, remained the best for over a century. He also made measurements of the heights of some of the lunar peaks, and although his results were naturally rough judged by modern standards, they were much more accurate than Galileo's.

Hevelius gave some thought to the best method of naming lunar features. He finally decided to give them terrestrial names, and this was the system followed in his map For instance, the crater now known as Copernicus was called 'Etna'; another large crater, the modern Plato, was 'The Greater Black Lake'. The whole system was feeble and clumsy, and only half a dozen of Hevelius' names are still in use.

There are still some copies of the map in existence, but the original copper-plate of it is no longer to be found. According to Señor Antonio Paluzíe-Borrell, the Spanish expert upon lunar history, it was made into a tea-pot after Hevelius' death!

Riccioli, an Italian priest, worked out a much better scheme of nomenclature. In 1651 he published a map in which each large crater was named in honour of a famous scientist or philosopher. Riccioli's motives have often been questioned, and it has been suggested that he adopted this system out of sheer vanity. Certainly he allotted large and important craters to himself and to his pupil, Grimaldi, upon whose observations the map was based; but, at any rate, his system soon replaced that of Hevelius, and nearly all of the names he gave (more than 200 in all) are still in use. Later astronomers have added to the list, and at the present time over 700 names are recognized, some of them those of living astronomers.[1]

[1] Among present-day astronomers commemorated in this way are K. W Abineri, D. P. Barcroft, R. Barker, Dr. J. Bartlett, C. Bertaud, D. W. G. Arthur,

No system can be completely satisfactory, and Riccioli's has its weaknesses. Some strange people seem to have found their way on to the moon. Julius Cæsar, certainly no scientist, is to be seen not far from the centre of the disk, and Alexander the Great and his friend Nearch also appear; there are even two Olympians, Atlas and Hercules. (One crater has been given the rather startling name of Hell. This does not, however, indicate any remarkable depth! It was named after Maximilian Hell, a Hungarian astronomer of the eighteenth century.) On the other hand, Riccioli 'gave away' all the largest and most important formations, so that later astronomers had to be content with second best. Thus we find Newton tucked away near the moon's South Pole, while Mädler, greatest of all lunar observers, is represented by a very insignificant crater on the Sea of Nectar.

Despite the abuse hurled at his head, Riccioli's idea was obviously a good one, and his system has stood the test of time. His map, however, was of very little use. It was not nearly so good as that of Hevelius, and but for his nomenclature would have been speedily forgotten.

The work of Schroter

For the next hundred years, little real progress was made in charting the lunar surface. At last, in 1775, a German astronomer named Tobias Mayer produced a comparatively accurate map 8 inches across, and this remained the best until just over a century ago; but true 'selenography' really began four years later, in 1779, when Johann Schröter founded a small private observatory at Lilienthal, near Bremen, and began to study the moon.

Schröter was not a professional astronomer. For many years he was the chief magistrate of Lilienthal, with ample means and leisure to carry on his hobby, and he collected several large telescopes–two made by William Herschel, the greatest instrument-maker of the age, and two even larger constructed by

R. M. Baum, E. E. Hare, Professor W. H Haas, A. Ingalls, A Paluzíe-Borrell, T. Sahekı, F. H Thornton and Dr H P. Wilkins Descartes, a seventeenth-century French philosopher, once made the cheerful statement that the spirits of those honoured by being placed on the moon went to reside in their own particular craters immediately after death. The above-mentioned astronomers, as well as the present writer, sincerely hope that such is not the case!

Schräder of Kiel, one of which had a 19-inch mirror. For thirty years he worked away, drawing, measuring and charting. To a great extent, he was breaking new ground; and it was he who first observed the deep cracks in the moon that we now call 'clefts'.

Schröter, like Riccioli, has been much maligned, and with even less reason. It is perfectly true that he was not a good draughtsman. His drawings are crude and schematic, and the detail is put in very clumsily. Some of his ideas, too, were strange; he believed that he had discovered important changes on the lunar surface, and he was prepared to admit that the moon was a world inhabited by intelligent beings. On the other hand he was a completely honest observer, and never drew anything unless he was certain he had seen it; and his height measurements were far better than those of his predecessors. He did not produce a complete map, but he did make thousands of drawings of different parts of the lunar surface; and his work has never really received sufficient credit except, perhaps, in Germany.

It is sad to relate that Schroter, most peaceful of men, became a victim of the Napoleonic Wars. In 1813, when he was sixty-eight years old, the French, under Vandamme, occupied Bremen; Lilienthal fell into their hands, and Schroter's observatory was burned to the ground, along with all his notes, manuscripts and unpublished observations. Even his brass-tubed telescopes were plundered by the French soldiers, who mistook them for gold; and the old astronomer, his life's work more or less wrecked, only lived for three years longer. The tragic destruction of the observatory at Lilienthal was sheer vandalism; yet can we, of the 'enlightened' twentieth century, afford to criticize? Between 1939 and 1945 European observatories, universities and libraries perished by the dozen. To take only one example, Pulkova Observatory, where the Struves worked for so long upon double-star measurements, was completely destroyed by the Germans during the siege of Leningrad, and is only now being rebuilt.

The mantle of Schröter fell upon three of his countrymen, Löhrmann, Beer and Mädler. All were clever draughtsmen as well as being good observers, and between them they explored every square mile of the moon's visible surface – but it must be remembered that they had Schröter's work to use as a basis. The credit for founding true 'lunar science' must go to the Lilienthal astronomer, and to him alone.

Lohrmann, and 'Der Mond'

Löhrmann, a land surveyor of Dresden, published a very accurate map 15 inches in diameter, and started out to construct a detailed chart over twice as large. Unfortunately he had only completed four sections when his eyesight failed him, and he had to give up. He died in 1840.

However, the most important work of the nineteenth century was done by a Berlin banker, Wilhelm Beer, and his friend, Dr. Johann Mädler. These two built an observatory at Beer's house, equipped it with a fine $3\frac{3}{4}$-inch refracting telescope, and studied the lunar surface patiently for over ten years, finally producing a map which has been the basis of all later studies. They followed it up with a book, *Der Mond*, which is a masterpiece of careful, accurate work. *Der Mond* appeared in 1838, and copies of it are still in existence, though unfortunately it has never been translated into English.

It is interesting to note that Mädler, who did nearly all the mapping, never used any telescope larger than a $3\frac{3}{4}$-inch refractor for his main lunar work. A refractor, which uses a lens to collect its light, is more powerful, inch for inch, than a reflector; but even so, the difference between Madler's instrument and Schröter's 19-inch is remarkable. It is true that Madler's probably gave a sharper image, but Schröter's extra aperture must have given him a distinct advantage when observing very faint details.

Beer and Mädler's work had a tremendous effect upon lunar studies, and, oddly enough, actually held them back to some extent. Schröter had believed the moon to be a living, changing world; Beer and Madler went to the other extreme, and considered that it was completely dead. Their opinions naturally carried a great deal of weight Neither of them did much more lunar work after 1840, when Mädler left Berlin to become Director of the Dorpat Observatory in Estonia, and nobody

else seemed inclined to take up the torch that they had thrown
down. The general opinion was that their map was the 'last
word' on the subject, and that as the moon was a changeless
world there was no point in observing it any further. Even now,
one or two astronomers hold similar views!

Whatever the cause, the quarter-century following the publi-
cation of *Der Mond* was totally non-productive. Observers had
turned their attentions elsewhere, and the Queen of Night, relegated to the status of a lifeless and uninteresting globe, was
shamefully neglected.

Schmidt

Luckily there was one astronomer, Julius Schmidt, who did
not agree. He began to observe the moon when he was still only
a boy, and continued to do so until he died in 1884. After acting
as assistant at various German observatories he was appointed
to the directorship of the Athens Observatory in 1858; and it
was in Greece that most of his lunar work was done.

Schmidt not only revised and completed the map begun by
Lóhrmann, but issued one of his own which will stand up to
comparison with the best modern charts Before this appeared,
however, much had happened, and Schmidt was primarily responsible. It was the 'Linné affair' which reawakened popular
interest in lunar study.

At various times, Lóhrmann, Beer and Mädler, and Schmidt
himself had recorded a deep crater in the Mare Serenitatis (Sea
of Serenity); Mädler had named it 'Linné' in honour of Carl
von Linné, the Swedish botanist. Then, in 1866, Schmidt announced that the crater was no longer there. It had, in fact,
vanished from the moon, or at least altered its appearance
beyond all recognition.

This was startling, to put it mildly. Could the moon be less
dead than Mädler had thought? It was a revolutionary idea, and
yet, coming from an observer with Schmidt's reputation, it
could not be disregarded. What Mädler's own views were is unfortunately unknown (he did not die until eight years later), but
at any rate the announcement did selenography a great deal of
good. Amateurs and professionals alike began to turn back to it,
and once more telescopes were pointed at the rocky, sphinx-like

lunar surface in an attempt to probe its secrets. Even now the Linné mystery has not been cleared up, and we shall return to it later, but if another change of equal importance takes place it will certainly run no risk of passing unnoticed.

The first British lunar maps

Up to eighty years ago, most of our knowledge of the moon's surface had been gleaned by German observers. Englishmen and Americans had done comparatively little, but this was altered during the last quarter of the nineteenth century

The first of the great English lunar works, written by Edmund Neison, appeared in 1876. Neison's map was not much more than a revision of Mädler's, but the book itself, containing a description of every named formation, was of tremendous value --in fact it still is, and even now copies can be picked up occasionally Just how much actual observation Neison himself did is not entirely clear, though it must have been considerable. He provides a link between the past and the present, he was only twenty-five when he wrote his book, and died as recently as 1938, although, amazingly, he seems to have taken no practical interest in the moon for the last sixty years of his life.

At about the time that Neison's book was published, a new society was formed in England, devoted entirely to the study of the moon. This was the Selenographical Society, and for ten years or so it was very active. In 1883, following the death of its president (W. R. Birt) and the resignation of its secretary (Neison), it was disbanded, but seven years later the newly formed British Astronomical Association established a lunar section and carried on its work.

From the start, the B.A.A has been made up primarily of amateurs; and since the moon is perhaps the one body in the heavens upon which valuable work can be done with small telescopes, there was no shortage of observers. Ever since 1890 the Lunar Section has kept up its activity, and eleven full-length Memoirs have been published, as well as dozens of papers and reports scattered through the sixty-four volumes of the B.A.A. *Journal.* Thomas Gwyn Elger, first Director of the Lunar Section, published a book on his own account in 1895, illustrated

D

by an outline map that remains probably the best of its kind.[1]

Photographing the moon

Meanwhile, the camera had begun to make its presence felt. The Daguerrotype process was discovered in 1839, and when Arago announced the invention to the French Academy of Sciences in the following year he showed that the importance of photography as applied to lunar study was not lost upon him. "By this means", he said, "we shall be able to accomplish one of the hardest tasks in astronomy – mapping the moon – in a few minutes." This forecast was certainly over-optimistic, but within twenty years Lewis Rutherfurd, in America, was taking photographs which revealed delicate detail, and in 1897 Loewy and Puiseux, at the Paris Observatory, produced a complete photographic atlas of the moon. A second followed in 1904, the work of Professor W. H. Pickering at the Jamaica station of the Harvard Observatory, showing each region of the moon under five different aspects of illumination.

Recent maps

Between 1900 and the end of the second World War, a great many lunar maps of various sizes and qualities were produced; but for the moment we need consider only two, those of Goodacre and Wilkins. Walter Goodacre, who succeeded Elger as Director of the B.A.A. Lunar Section, published a 77-inch map in 1910, and twenty years later followed it up with a book containing a reduced edition of the map. Both are of great value, but unfortunately very difficult to obtain. The book was privately printed at Bournemouth, and only a few hundred copies of it were made; obviously these soon ran out, and as no more were printed the book is now extremely scarce.

However, all previous maps have been more or less superseded by that of Dr. H. P. Wilkins, the present Director of the B.A.A. Lunar Section. Dr. Wilkins began lunar work in 1909. His first map, issued in 1924, had a diameter of 60 inches, and was followed by a gigantic chart 300 inches across. The third edition of this, reduced to a scale of 100 inches to the moon's

[1] Elger's map, revised by Dr Wilkins, has recently been reprinted, and is easily obtainable. The book, unfortunately, is out of print.

diameter, appeared in 1951. It has been constructed from the best available photographs and measures, as well as thousands of personal observations by its author, and its accuracy cannot possibly be questioned, so that it is likely to remain the standard map until surveys can be carried out from the lunar surface itself. Moreover, it actually covers more of the moon than any of its predecessors. All other maps have been drawn to 'mean libration', a term which requires some explanation. As we have seen, the moon does not keep exactly the same face permanently towards the earth; the various librations make it sway slightly, so that sometimes one limb is uncovered, sometimes another. 'Mean libration' is the position in which all four limbs are equally exposed. A special chart in Dr. Wilkins' map shows each limb under its most favourable libration, and thus covers all the four-sevenths of the surface available to us. The book to accompany the map, containing a detailed description of the entire moon, is at present being written, and will appear within the next year or so.

Observers of to-day

At the present time, lunar studies are being carried on in all parts of the world. British observers are certainly very active. During the war years the B.A A. Lunar Section was able to do little, but by 1947, following the appointment of Dr. Wilkins as Director, was in full working order again, with a membership of over 100; and recently two full-length Memoirs and numerous papers and reports have been issued. Many of its members work with comparatively modest equipment, but the 18-inch reflector used by F. H. Thornton, of Northwich, is probably the largest in the world employed almost solely upon lunar work (though Dr. Wilkins is at present constructing a 22-inch); and among other British observers engaged upon systematic work with large telescopes may be mentioned Robert Barker, of Cheshunt; K. W. Abineri, of London; L. F. Ball, of Guildford (who has been responsible for Plates III, IV and VI of this book); E. A. Whitaker, of Greenwich Observatory; R. M. Baum, of Chester; and D. W. G. Arthur, of Wokingham.

American observers are equally energetic. The Association of Lunar and Planetary Observers, founded by Professor W. H.

Haas after the end of the recent war, comprises a large number of skilled amateurs and professionals paying great attention to the moon's surface.

In Japan, the Oriental Astronomical Association has an active lunar section; and work is also going on in Germany, France, Spain and many other countries. In fact, the moon is the business not of one nation, but of all nations, and results and observations are exchanged and compared with perfect freedom. Let us hope that this spirit stays with us when the time comes for man to take his first voyage into the depths of space.

Why do we observe the moon?

It is clear enough why so much time has been spent in mapping the smaller details of the moon's surface. The first interplanetary travellers will need not only accurate charts, but also a working knowledge of the conditions they are likely to find; for this, they will have to turn to astronomers–and, to a large extent, to amateur astronomers. The great observatories of the world, Palomar, Lick and the rest, use their giant telescopes principally to explore the remote parts of the universe far beyond the reach of smaller instruments, and it is seldom that they pay any attention to the moon. There are exceptions to this rule–for instance, the photographs taken at the Pic du Midi Observatory far surpass any obtained before, and show details only a few yards across–but in general, lunar study is left to the amateurs. The fact that Mädler produced his classic map with the aid of only a tiny telescope is proof of the fact that patience, keen sight and good draughtsmanship will work wonders.

This review of 'the observers of the moon' is very sketchy and incomplete, but if we are to form a complete picture of lunar science we must know a little, at least, about what has gone before. Mayer, Schröter, Mädler and the rest are not mere voices from the past; their work lives on. Only by checking their observations against our own can we track down the minute changes which take place upon the moon's rugged surface, showing us that the Queen of Night is far from being the dull, inert body that Mädler thought her to be.

CHAPTER 6

FEATURES OF THE MOON

WHEN we first look at the moon through a telescope, the whole surface seems a tangled confusion, so crowded with detail that any attempt to map it seems doomed to failure. Before long, however, the impression wears off, and a good deal of order begins to emerge from the outward chaos. In particular, the various features sort themselves out into well-defined types; and a few evenings at the telescope—or, for that matter, studying photographs—will lead to quick recognition of the chief lunar features.

There are over 700 surface formations considered important enough to be worthy of separate names, and the total number of recorded features amounts to rather more than 100,000, so that to describe them all would require a very large book. However, we can at least indicate some of the more interesting objects, and the folded map will be helpful.

The outline map

This map was constructed from three photographs, and does not pretend to be anything more than an outline. It is not easy to strike a happy mean between ultra-simplification and over-crowding, but generally speaking the most conspicuous formations have been named, together with some less obvious ones which have points of special interest (such as the celebrated Linné).

The first noticeable thing about the map is that it is drawn with south at the top and north at the bottom. This may seem curious, but astronomical pictures are always turned round in this way. A telescope gives a naturally inverted image, and to correct this for terrestrial use an extra lens is introduced. Every time a light-ray passes through a lens it becomes slightly enfeebled, and although this does not matter in the least normally, it is important to collect all possible light from the comparatively faint celestial bodies. In astronomical telescopes, therefore, the correcting lens is left out, and all views are obtained upside-down. There is no other essential difference between the astronomical refractor and the ordinary naval telescope, and binoculars are constructed in just the same way.

The map is of course drawn to mean libration (though on this scale the difference for any particular limb is almost inappreciable), and for convenience divided into four quadrants, the first being north-west, the second the north-east, the third the south-east and the fourth the south-west.

Lighting effects

The beginner is often confused by the rapid changes in surface appearance caused by the changing lighting. It is true that a peak or crater can alter almost beyond recognition in only a few hours, and this is because we depend so much on shadows. When the sun is rising or setting on an elevation, the shadow cast is long and prominent; when the sun is high over it, the shadow becomes very short or vanishes completely--just as we can see the shadow of a tree or post shortening as the sun rises over it--and as there is no local colour on the moon the elevation will not be visible at all unless it is definitely brighter or darker than the surrounding country. This effect is even more noticeable for the craters. To see a walled formation properly it must be caught when it is on or near the 'terminator', an expression which needs some explanation.

The terminator is the boundary between the day and night sides of the moon. It must not be confused with the 'limb', which is the moon's apparent edge as seen from the earth. The limb remains in almost the same position; and although it does shift slightly, owing to the various librations, the effect is hardly perceptible except in areas close to it. On the other hand the terminator sweeps right across the disk twice each lunation, first when the moon is waxing ('morning terminator') and then when it is waning ('evening terminator'), so that even an hour's watch will reveal definite movement. In Fig. 5 the full, gibbous, half and crescent phases of the moon are shown, with the limb drawn as a continuous line and the terminator dotted.

Owing to the roughness of the lunar surface, the terminator does not appear as a smooth line. As the sun rises, the first rays naturally catch the mountain-tops and higher areas before the depressions and crater-floors, so that the terminator presents very jagged and uneven appearance. Peaks glitter like stars out of the blackness, while their bases are still shrouded in night, appearing completely detached from the shining part of the moon; ridges make their first appearance in the guise of luminous threads, while a crater will show its rampart-crests and the top of its central mountain while its floor is still perfectly black. On the other hand, a low-lying area will appear as a great dent in the terminator and take on a false importance for a few hours. Even with a small telescope, it is fascinating to watch the slow, steady progress of sunrise upon the bleak lunar landscape.

The result of this is that the features shown on the map cannot be seen all at the same time. In fact, it is more or less true to say that the full moon is the worst possible time for observ-

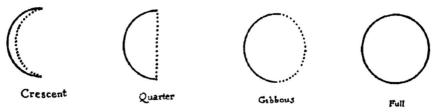

Crescent   Quarter   Gibbous   Full

Fig. 5. THE TERMINATOR

ing, as the limb appears complete all round the disk and shadows are at their minimum.[1] Moreover, the strong ash-rays drown most of the detail, causing the moon to take on the appearance and of a blurred, speckled circle of confused light. The full moon and crescent moon photographs (frontispiece and Plate I) demonstrate this very well.

The lunar 'seas'

Of course, the vast dark plains known as the 'seas' catch the eye at once. They take up half the visible disk, and cover most of the eastern hemisphere—which explains why the 'last quarter' moon, when the eastern side is shining by itself, is less brilliant than the 'first quarter' moon, when the western half is visible.

There are nine important seas and a number of lesser ones,

[1] Certain more delicate observations are, of course, best carried out when the formation concerned is under high light; but the appearance is not nearly so spectacular, particularly in the case of a crater.

although nearly all of these are combined into one great connected system, as are our own water-oceans, and there are often
no hard-and-fast boundaries. On first acquaintance, the names
are perhaps rather confusing. Latin is still the universal language, and therefore astronomers use Latin rather than English
names; the Sea of Showers becomes 'Mare Imbrium', the Sea
of Vapours 'Mare Vaporum'.[1] Other names are even more
romantic -for instance we have a Sea of Nectar, a Bay of Rainbows and an Ocean of Storms -but we have to admit that they
are rather inappropriate. Showers, rainbows, nectar and storms
are very much out of place on the glaring, tangled rocks of the
lunar world.

The seas, with their Latin names and English equivalents, are
listed opposite the map. The Latin versions are used for all
lunar charts, and it will be better for us to keep to them here.

We know, of course, that there is no water on the moon now,
and that the 'seas' are dry plains without a trace of moisture in
them. Once, earlier in lunar history, they may well have been
seas of lava, although it does not seem likely that they were ever
filled with water. At any rate, it is quite certain that they were
still liquid long after the rest of the surface had become permanently rigid. This is shown by their treatment of the mountains and craters bordering them. We can see traces of the old
wall between the Mare Humorum and the Mare Nubium (third
quadrant), and coastal craters have had their seaward walls
breached and levelled. Water could have been responsible; all
of us have seen the gradual wearing-away and destruction of a
boy's sand-castle as the incoming tide laps over it. From what
we know about the past history of the moon, however, it seems
much more likely that the destroying agent was liquid lava.

Many of the seas are more or less circular, and bordered by
high mountain ranges. Look, for instance, at the most impressive of all-the Mare Imbrium, or Sea of Showers, in the second
quadrant. It appears oval in shape, but this is because it is
foreshortened; really it is almost circular, made up of four lofty
mountain ranges hemming in a lava plain large enough to hold
England and France put together. The even larger Oceanus

---

[1] 'Mare', pronounced Mah-ri, is the Latin word for sea; plural, Maria. Ocean
is 'oceanus', bay 'sinus', marsh 'palus' and lake 'lacus'.

Procellarum (Ocean of Storms), further south, is less regular in shape, and does not show the same steely tint; it is lighter and patchier, which seems to indicate that its lava-layer is not so thick. Indeed, only the Mare Serenitatis and the smaller, isolated Mare Crisium are so regular in form as the Mare Imbrium, and some of the other 'seas' are probably mere surface deposits, not genuine Maria at all.

J. E. Spurr, an American geologist who has paid a great deal of attention to the moon, has christened the bright upland material 'lunarite' and the dark Mare-material 'lunabase', two names which seem eminently suitable and will probably come into general use. Lunabase is not, however, confined entirely to the seas. Some craters have their floors covered with it, and there are also small 'splashes' of it here and there in the uplands.

The mountains of the moon

The bright mountainous areas, found chiefly in the southern part of the moon, are packed with detail. Peaks, craters, valleys and ridges jostle against each other in a wild tangle, leaving hardly a square yard of level ground. Space-craft of the future will be hard put to it to find any suitable landing-stations there.

Although the surface of the moon is now peaceful, silent and almost undisturbed, there must have been a time when it was the scene of tremendous volcanic activity. In those remote days giant volcanoes roared into the sky, and the molten, steaming lunar surface was hammered by falling rocks and scorched by burning ashes, while the crust twisted and heaved as mighty eruptions tore it apart. The result of this was that when all activity died down, high mountains were left on the surface.

The moon is smaller than the earth, and if the mountains were no higher relatively than ours they would only rise to some 6,000 feet—less than twice the height of Scafell, in Cumberland. Actually they tower to more than the height of Mount Everest, earth's loftiest peak. The highest of all the mountains of the moon, the Leibnitz (near the South Pole) rise to something like 35,000 feet; but it is difficult to give the heights with real accuracy, because we have no standard of reference. On the earth we use sea-level, but there is no water on the moon, and the best we can do is to measure the summit-heights of the mountains above the lower-lying country near their bases.

If Everest were as high, relative to the earth, as the loftiest Leibnitz peaks are relative to the moon, it would rise 20 miles into our stratosphere, where the sky is greyish-black and hurricanes rend the thin, ice-cold air.

As a matter of fact the Leibnitz Mountains themselves do not look at all impressive, because they are so badly placed. They lie right on the lunar limb, and can never be seen well. Much more spectacular are the Apennines, which form the south-east boundary of the great Mare Imbrium. The range is over 400 miles long, and some of the peaks rise to 20,000 feet, far higher than Mont Blanc or the loftiest summits of the Rockies. When well-placed the range is a magnificent spectacle, with its massive, towering mountains gleaming against the greyness of the plain. The chain is interrupted by broad valleys; narrow rifts thread the foothills, and here and there craters can be seen, hemmed in on all sides.

No earthly scenery can compare with the wild grandeur of the lunar Apennines. The first lunar mountaineers will need many years to explore their hidden wonders—wonders which we, from our distance of a quarter of a million miles, can already begin to appreciate; and the conquest of Mount Huygens, king of the range, will be a feat far more notable than that of mastering our own Himalayas.

The first exploration of the summit of Mount Everest, the highest of all terrestrial mountains, was carried out from an aeroplane; but nothing of the kind will be possible in the case of the lunar Apennines. Aeroplanes and helicopters will not function on the airless moon, and rockets are unreliable and inefficient at low speeds. The smaller force of gravity will prove a distinct advantage to mountaineers, but will be offset to some extent by the necessity of wearing cumbersome space-suits.

The shadows thrown by lunar peaks are long and slender, showing that the peaks themselves are very sharp. Terrestrial mountains are rounded and blunted by erosion, the action of wind and water; but on the almost airless and completely waterless moon there is no such erosion, and the peaks remain in their original jagged state. There is one curious range, however, which seems to form an exception to the rule The low and inconspicuous Riphæn Mountains, in the Mare Nubium or Sea of Clouds (third quadrant, not far from the equator), seem oddly rounded, as though they had undergone centuries of weathering. It is absurd to suppose that one minor range, and one only, has suffered in this way, and there can be no doubt that the appearance is misleading. Whatever caused the wearing-down of the Riphæn peaks, it was neither wind nor water. Perhaps it was the Mare lava itself which hammered against the once lofty mountains, destroying most of them and reducing the rest to the low, worn hills which we now see as the Riphæns.

Valleys

Wherever there are mountains there will be valleys, and this is so on the moon some mere passes, others wide rifts in the rugged chains. One of them, the Rheita valley in the fourth quadrant, is long enough to stretch from London to Birmingham, and looks almost as though it had been scooped out by a gigantic chisel, though it is really made up of a number of craters which have run together.

The wedge-shaped valley of the Alps, near the dark-floored crater Plato on the north-west border of the Mare Imbrium, is even more striking. Over 80 miles long, it looks as though it had been carved out by a great rock crashing through the mountains, though this cannot really be so because there are smaller parallel valleys to either side of it. In the future it may well be used as a highway between the Mare Imbrium and the lunar arctic; for the present, it remains one of the more puzzling features of the moon. Some people have compared it to the Grand Cañon of the Colorado, though it is quite certain that its formation was not due to the action of water.

Peaks

As well as the great ranges, there are many isolated mountains on the moon. In the uplands they are to be found in hundreds, but those on the seas are far more impressive, as they stand out as glittering points against the greyness They are not generally so lofty as the peaks of the great chains; but all the same, some of them would rank with the famous mountains of our own planet.

Look, for instance, at Pico on the Mare Imbrium, 100 miles south of Plato, a mountain mass with broad slopes cut by hundreds of crevasses, and foothills studded with pits and craterlets. It may not look impressive on the map, but the highest of its three summit-peaks rises to a good 8,000 feet above the plain, so that it is twice the height of Scotland's much-vaunted Ben Nevis.

Less important peaks are correspondingly more common, and indeed the whole moon is dotted with hills, many of them no more than mere mounds. Even the floors of the craters are not free from them, and the smoothest parts of the sea-beds are very far from flat, although it is naturally difficult to recognize slight differences in level unless we catch them under a very low sun.

We should not regard the English Fens as very level if we came across a 20-foot mound or a pronounced crater-pit every few dozen yards; but no part of the lunar surface is any smoother than this. This is hardly surprising, in view of the tremendous volcanic forces that were unleashed there in past ages; and it must be remembered that there has been no weathering to wear down the elevations, as has been the case on earth.

Measuring the lunar peaks

The first to make a serious effort to measure the heights of the lunar mountains was Galileo. As the sun rises, a mountain-top will catch the first rays before the lower-lying country round, and so will appear as a bright point detached from the bright body of the moon. All Galileo did was to observe how long the mountain remained illuminated on the 'night' side of the terminator, after which its distance from the terminator, and therefore its height, could be worked out by ordinary trigonometry.

Unfortunately the terminator is so irregular, owing to the moon's uneven surface, that its position cannot be measured with any accuracy; consequently, Galileo's results were very inexact. It is true that he did give altitudes of around 33,000 feet for some peaks, and this would have been correct for the

Leibnitz or the almost equally lofty Dörfels (third quadrant), but these were not the ranges which Galileo measured. He seems to have concentrated on the Apennines and Caucasus, which are much lower, and his stated heights are nearly double the true values.

The present method is to measure the shadow cast by the peak itself. The position of the peak is known, and so is the angle at which the solar rays strike it, so that the height relative to the neighbouring surface can be calculated (Fig. 6). Of course,

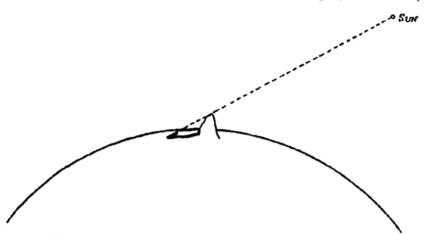

Fig. 6. MEASURING THE HEIGHT OF A LUNAR MOUNTAIN

there are several complications to be taken into account; but the method itself is perfectly straightforward.

The lunar domes

Closely related to the isolated peaks, perhaps forming a link between them and the craters, are the curious formations known as 'domes'. As their name suggests, they are surface bubbles or swellings, and give the impression that they were produced by some internal force pushing up the crust without being able to break it. They bear some superficial resemblance in form to the bubbles seen in boiling porridge.

Domes are not nearly so rare as was believed until recently, but only a few dozen are known as yet, and as they are low and often hemmed in by rough ground they are very easy to overlook. They escaped notice for many years, but in 1932 Robert

Barker, one of the best-known of modern English lunar observers, drew attention to them by pointing out the existence of a particularly good specimen inside the large, ruined walled plain Darwin (third quadrant, near the limb), which he described as "a huge cinder-heap, a lunarian dust-heap which bristles with roughness–like a selenite slag-heap".

Strangely enough, all domes appear dark when the sun is low over them. There must be a good reason for this behaviour, and Dr. S. R. B. Cooke, who has made a special study of them, suggests that they are seamed with minute fissures which are shadow-filled under oblique lighting, causing the whole dome area to appear dark. This fits in very well with Barker's description of the Darwin dome, and is almost certainly the correct explanation.

Faults and ridges

The upland areas of the moon are so rugged that it is difficult to make out even well-defined geological faults, but on the Mare Nubium, west of the conspicuous crater Bullialdus (third quadrant), we find a remarkable formation known as the Straight Wall–well shown in the beautiful drawing by L. F. Ball (Plate III). It is not happily named, as it is not completely straight and is certainly not a wall! It is in fact a vast fault; the plain to the east drops suddenly by some 800 feet, forming a magnificent line of cliffs some 60 miles long, compared to which the 'white cliffs of Dover' would seem very insignificant. At the southern end of the cliff-line lie some clumps of hills, known as the Stag's-Horn Mountains.

Although there are few major mountain ranges on the Mare surfaces, there are plenty of ridges, some of which run for hundreds of miles and form complex, branching systems. In many areas the whole surface is threaded with them, and some of the large craters seem to be the centres of radiating ridge-systems.

The craters of the moon

We now come to the walled formations, which dominate the entire surface of the moon. No area is free from them; the smoothest portions of the plains, the wildest regions of the mountains, and even the summits of peaks contain the circular pits, with raised walls and sunken floors, that we call the lunar 'craters'.

As a matter of fact, the name is distinctly unfortunate. If we take the word in its terrestrial sense, the formations are not true craters at all, even though they are certainly volcanic in nature. They are better termed 'walled depressions', for although their ramparts tower above their floors, the level of the highest wall-crests is often not much above that of the outside country. Moreover, they are incomparably vaster than the puny craters of our own world. The famous craters of Vesuvius would cut a very poor figure if transferred to the moon, and would certainly not be honoured with separate names. Quite apart from this, a lunar crater is so different in form from a terrestrial one that it can be regarded only as a 'distant relation'.[1]

When we measure the 'depth' of a crater, what we mean is

Fig. 7. CROSS-SECTION OF THE LUNAR CRATER THÆTETUS
(The curvature of the lunar surface is neglected)

the height of the rampart above the floor; and this gives the impression that the wall is much loftier than it really is. Let us consider the crater Thætetus, on the Mare Imbrium (second quadrant), shown in cross-section in Fig. 7. It is 16 miles across, so that it would be large enough to hold the Isle of Wight, and the walls rise to 7,000 feet above the interior This sounds a considerable height, but the floor itself is 5,000 feet below the outer plain, so that an observer standing on the Mare Imbrium looking at Thætetus' outer rim would be confronted only with a modest-looking range of hills much lower than Scafell Only when he climbed the peaks and looked over them would he see them in their true guise.

It is also a fact that an observer standing inside a lunar crater would not have much impression of depth. The average crater is much more like a flat dish than a bucket, and this too is clear from the cross-section of Thætetus. The moon's surface curves

[1] Shaler's alternative term 'vulcanoid' has much to recommend it, and it is rather surprising that it has not come into general use.

more sharply than the earth's, so that the horizon is correspondingly nearer, and if we stood in the middle of Plato, a
crater 60 miles across with ramparts higher than Ben Nevis, we
should hardly be able to see the walls at all. Our first ideas of
lunar craters as deep, gaping holes in the surface, banked with
mountains which rise sheer from the shadowed depths, will
have to be drastically revised.

It has often been stated that if one digs a hole, piling the
excavated material evenly around the edge, the result will be
similar in form to a lunar crater. There is certainly some
analogy, as the 'walls' of the hole will rise to some distance
above the bottom, even though they are very low above the
level of the surrounding ground.

There is one factor common to all the craters, large and
small. All are basically circular, even though they may have
been battered and distorted by later eruptions. As the principal
seas are also circular, there seems after all to be no fundamental
difference between the two types of formation.

The craters away from the centre of the disk appear to us as
ovals, but this is merely an optical effect, due to foreshortening.
For instance, the great crater Gauss, in the first quadrant, is
actually circular, but so near the limb that it appears as a long
ellipse. In the 'libration areas', at the limit of our view, it
becomes very difficult to map the features at all accurately, and
it is often impossible to tell whether an object is a foreshortened
crater or merely a ridge.

The walled plains

The largest craters, more suitably termed 'walled plains', are
also the oldest, as they were produced by the tremendous upheavals in the early days when the moon was at its most violent.
Many of them are now so broken and ruined that they are
scarcely recognizable. For instance, Janssen, in the fourth
quadrant not far from the Mare Australe, must once have been
a noble object, with high continuous walls rising to thousands
of feet above its sunken floor; but it has been so roughly treated
by later eruptions and crustal disturbances that it is now no
more than an immense field of ruins, broken by craters, ridges,
pits and clefts, with its walls breached in dozens of places and

completely levelled in some. Only when it is right on the terminator, and filled with shadow, does it give a faint impression of its former self.

However, quite a number of the walled plains have managed to escape relatively unharmed—such as Clavius, in the rough southern uplands, which is large enough to contain the whole of Switzerland, and has walls towering 17,000 feet above its sunken amphitheatre.

Newton, near the South Pole, is even deeper. Its loftiest crest is some 29,000 feet above the floor, so that if we put Mount Everest inside the hollow only the extreme tip would poke out. Moreover, because Newton is so deep, and so near the Pole, neither sun nor earth can ever be seen from parts of its interior; the ice-cold rocks have lain undisturbed for millions of years, and eternal blackness and silence must reign there, where no friendly gleam can penetrate. The bottom of Newton must be one of the most desolate spots in the whole solar system. We cannot form any real picture of what it must be like—even if we grope our way into the far tunnels of some great grotto, and stand there alone.

One or two walled plains are notable for the darkness of their floors. For instance Plato, on the northern border of the Mare Imbrium—large enough to hold Devonshire comfortably—has a steel-grey amphitheatre, probably the most level spot on the whole moon. An even darker walled plain is Grimaldi, near the east limb, whose iron-grey floor can be recognized under any conditions of illumination.

Before leaving the walled plains, let us note their tendency to arrange themselves in lines. A chain of tremendous formations runs down the western limb, from Furnerius, near the Mare Australe, as far as the dark-floored Endymion in the north, and even more striking lines of plains can be seen near the centre of the disk. When well placed, the three great formations Ptolemæus, Alphons and Arzachel (third quadrant) are particularly imposing.

The smaller craters

Coming now to the smaller craters, we find that they can be divided broadly into two classes: those with central peaks, and

E

those without. Some craters have mountains which tower to heights of thousands of feet, though they never attain the height of the surrounding rampart, others have lower, many-peaked central elevations, and sometimes the so-called central mountain is little more than a low mound. There are even formations which have central craterlets instead of peaks, while sometimes the entire floor is featureless except for low hummocks and pits

Rather than describe several craters, it will be better to select one, Copernicus in the Oceanus Procellarum, which shows many of the features seen in its lesser companions.

The 'monarch of the moon'

Copernicus has massive mountain walls rising to 17,000 feet above the inner amphitheatre. The distance right across the crater, from crest to crest, is 56 miles, but the true 'floor' is only 40 miles across—the rest of it is blocked with rubble and débris resulting from huge landslides from the ramparts. Copernicus seems calm enough now, after its millions of years' silence; but we can picture the tumult, the pandemonium, the thunder of the boulders as they crashed down in past ages. Truly, the moon has had a troubled history.

The central heights are made up of three distinct, many-peaked masses, while lower hills and tangled rocks litter the whole area of the floor. The outer slopes of the walls are comparatively gentle, and lined with valleys and lava-ridges which radiate outwards. Similar gullies are seen near other craters, and Spurr has suggested that they were formed by water pouring down the outer slopes from the crater orifice, much in the way that narrow channels are formed in a sand-bank when water is poured down it; but this explanation is not generally accepted, owing to the difficulties in the way of supposing that large quantities of water ever existed on the moon.

Another feature of Copernicus is the terracing of the inner walls, and this again is very common among lunar craters. It is well shown in Plate IV for Bullialdus, a noble crater in the Mare Nubium, which bears a marked resemblance to Copernicus. Sometimes there are three or four terraces, separated by yawning ravines, and just occasionally a complete concentric inner ring—a crater within a crater, so to speak.

It is impossible to do justice to Copernicus by written description. Even in a small telescope it is a superb sight, and the more it is studied the more wonders will it reveal. Well has it been nicknamed 'the monarch of the moon'.

Ruined craters

Copernicus was obviously formed fairly late in the moon's history, when the Mare lava had more or less solidified; but older craters were not so lucky. Those on the sea-coasts had their seaward walls broken down and levelled, so that the formations have been turned into huge bays; sometimes the ruins of a seaward wall can still be seen, sometimes even the wreck of a central mountain.

The most splendid of the bays is the Sinus Iridum (Bay of Rainbows), leading off the Mare Imbrium. The ground-level drops gradually to the east, and low, discontinuous remnants of the old west wall can still be traced between the two jutting capes that bound the strait separating the bay from the main mare. When the terminator passes close by, the mountain peaks of the eastern border (the Juras) catch the light, and the whole bay stands out from the blackness like a handle studded with gleaming jewels.

Old craters right on the seas have been even more unfortunate, and have been 'drowned' in the rising, flowing lava, so that they now appear veritable ghosts—marked sometimes by low, discontinuous walls, sometimes by nothing more than a slight change in the colour of the plain.

Look for instance at Stadius, in the Mare Nubium. It is large enough to hold the whole county of Sussex, and must once have been a noble formation, but nowadays it is in a sad state. The all-destroying lava has flowed across it, breaching the ramparts and leaving them shattered and ruined. The loftiest summits cannot now be more than a couple of hundred feet above the plain, and for long stretches the wall cannot be traced at all, while the amphitheatre has been filled up and speckled with hundreds upon hundreds of tiny pits. Unless it is caught under very oblique lighting, it is difficult to find. Its neighbour Eratosthenes, only about 100 miles off, has escaped completely, and must have been born far later than the crater whose pathetic remnants we now call Stadius.

We can go back once more to our boy digging in the sand. Suppose that he digs two holes, each time piling the sand in a ring–one at the point reached by the highest tide, and the other lower down the beach The first formation will have its seaward wall broken and its floor flooded, as Fracastorius and Sinus Iridum have been; the second will be overwhelmed by the rising ocean, and may be compared to old Stadius.

Twin craters

The arrangement of the craters calls for some comment. Like the great plains, they tend to line up, and also frequently appear in pairs, sometimes separate, sometimes joined together so that one 'twin' has been damaged by the other. Moreover, there is no known case of a lunar crater breaking into a smaller one. The big formations always come off worst, and this is only to be expected, as the large craters were formed early in lunar history when the activity was at its most violent. The smaller craters came later, and were able to damage their older brothers with impunity.

Craterlets

Craterlets, with diameters ranging from a dozen miles down to only a few yards, pepper the whole moon Some are complete miniatures of the larger craters, even to the central hill; others are mere pits, with depressed floors and steep walls which rise little if at all, above the outer surface. Spurr has called these latter objects 'blowhole-craters', and the name seems very appropriate.

A lunar plateau

Finally, let us note a real lunar freak–the celebrated plateau Wargentin, shown on the photograph (Plate VI) close to the large walled plain Schickard. Here the floor is not sunken, but raised above the outer surface by over 1,000 feet. What must have happened is that some blockage caused the molten lava to be trapped inside the amphitheatre when the crater had only just been formed, so that instead of subsiding and flowing away, as was usually the case, the lava solidified where it was. The true 'floor' of Wargentin is therefore hidden, and all we can see is the top of the deep lava-lake. In places the lava is level with the top of the old rampart, but in others there are still traces of a wall—one segment rises to as much as 500 feet. Still, the general impression is that of a flat tableland, and not a crater at all. Wargentin is large enough to hold the whole of Lancashire, and it is a great pity that it is not nearer the centre of the disk, as there are no other plateaux anything like so large.

It has been necessary to spend some time describing the various crater forms, as the walled formations dominate the entire lunar surface. Even the briefest description of the moon without paying due attention to them would be about as appropriate as acting *Hamlet* without introducing the Prince of Denmark.

The clefts

Let us now pass on to the deep cracks or 'clefts', first observed a century and a half ago by the ill-fated Schröter.

Here, as with the craters, appearances are deceptive. There is a temptation to regard the clefts as analogous to terrestrial rivers; but although lunar and earthly craters have at least vulcanism in common, there is no relationship at all between the clefts of the moon and the rivers of the earth, despite the fact that some of the true clefts are deep and steep-sided, bearing a superficial resemblance to gorges. One or two are of great length. The Ariadæus Cleft, in the Mare Vaporum (first quadrant, near the centre of the disk) can be seen in any small telescope, and is long enough to stretch from London to Manchester, while the great Herodotus valley-cleft, near the crater of that name in the Oceanus Procellarum, is even finer; it starts inside the crater as a thin crack, broadens out to a lagoon-like formation known as the Cobra-Head,[1] and winds across the plain as a tremendous valley, ending in a small craterlet. Its depth is something like 1,500 feet.

The clefts are by no means moonwide. Vast areas lack them completely; on the other hand some regions are criss-crossed with them, and there may be dozens within a hundred square

[1] A name due to Dr. W. H. Steavenson, Gresham Professor in Astronomy.

miles There are also one or two large walled plains with cleft-riddled floors.

As the clefts are steep and narrow, their bottoms are usually shrouded in shadow, causing them to appear as dark lines. Sometimes, however, a cleft running over the terminator can be seen prolonged into the blackness as a bright line. This is because many clefts have raised banks, and these banks naturally catch the sunlight when still on the night-side, just as ordinary ridges do.

Crater-chains

One of the most conspicuous of the clefts, that associated with the craterlet Hyginus in the Mare Vaporum, seems to be made up of a row of craters which have merged into each other with the loss of their dividing walls–so that it can hardly be

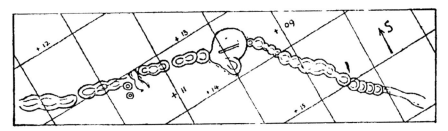

Fig. 8. THE HYGINUS CLEFT AS A CRATER-CHAIN

called a genuine cleft at all. This is well shown in the sketch by D. W G. Arthur (Fig. 8). A small telescope certainly does show the cleft in the guise of a gaping ravine, but higher powers at once reveal tell-tale bulges all along it.

Hyginus makes us rather suspicious If one of the greatest 'clefts' turns out to be nothing more than a crater-chain, what about the others ? This question has often been asked; but there can be no doubt that most of the clefts are true cracks in the lunar surface, similar to those shown in L. F. Ball's drawing of the region near Torricelli, a curious little formation in the southernmost part of the Mare Tranquillitatis (Plate VII). They bear a marked resemblance to the cracks seen in hard mud or clay.

On the other hand, there are plenty of crater-chains which cannot possibly be mistaken for clefts. No long ago the writer was mapping a small area not far from Wargéntin, and found no less than four distinct crater-chains within 100 miles. After all, there is nothing surprising in this. The great plains arrange themselves in lines; why should not the smaller ones do likewise? Once more we have a complete series from the 'giants' down to the 'strings of beads'.

The bright rays

Finally, something must be said about the lunar rays, certainly the most puzzling features of the moon's face. Like the sphinx, the Queen of Night is slow to yield up her secrets, and it does not seem likely that we shall fathom the true nature of the rays until we actually set foot upon the lunar surface. However, we can at least speculate about them.

Unlike most other details, the rays are best seen under high light. In fact, they are totally invisible when close to the terminator, and only begin to show when the sun has risen to some height above them. Of the dozens of ray-systems on the surface, two stand out as incomparably more splendid than the rest - those associated with the craters Tycho and Copernicus. Both are well shown on the full moon photograph.

Tycho is a conspicuous crater in the southern uplands, 54 miles across and with high terraced walls rising to some 17,000 feet above the amphitheatre. There is also a central peak. Magnificent though it is, Tycho lies in a crowded area, and would not be particularly remarkable were it not for the rays. When it first emerges from the lunar night, it appears to be a perfectly normal, rather bright crater. Gradually the rays start to show, and by full moon they dominate not only the surrounding area, but the whole of that part of the disk. There are dozens upon dozens of them, streaking out in all directions from Tycho as a focal point, they cross craters, peaks and valleys, uplands and maria, clefts and pits without deviating one iota from their course.

Strange to say, the rays cannot be followed right into Tycho There is a 'ray-free' area round the rampart, showing darkish under a high light, where they stop short. However, there can be no doubt that whatever the exact nature of the rays, Tycho is responsible for them.

The rays associated with Copernicus are rather different from those of Tycho. They are not so brilliant, and at full moon, when they are best seen, appear rather less bright than the gleaming crater-ring of Copernicus itself; neither are they so long, though they spread widely over the surrounding plain. Here and there, all over the disk, other smaller ray-centres can be made out.

It is easy to see that the rays are not continuous white streaks. When closely examined they are seen to possess definite structure, and so cannot be surface cracks or anything of the sort—though this is perfectly obvious in any case, from the way in which they cross all other types of formations and drown them in light.

Reports of shadows cast by rays have been received from time to time, but none have been confirmed, and it is impossible to doubt that the rays are due to some sort of deposit on the lunar surface. Salts have been suggested, but on the whole ash seems to be the best answer, although just why the streamers are so long and so straight is still a mystery. The ash theory is supported by other less conspicuous ray-systems, where the streamers are grey, not brilliant white, and so like the surrounding surface in hue that they are difficult to make out at all.

We have now reviewed at least some of the interesting features of the lunar surface. Much remains unsaid; but here, as in most other things, an ounce of practice is worth a ton of theory. The amateur who takes even a small telescope and turns it towards the moon, will find so many wonders open to his inspection that he will be quite unable to take them all in at once – particularly when he reflects that his children, or at any rate his children's children, may well have the chance to tread the bleak lunar rocks and explore for themselves.

CHAPTER 7

THE NATURE OF THE SURFACE

ON a clear winter's night, the moon shines down from the heavens with a brilliant radiance that floods the landscape with light and throws long black shadows on the earth, drowning the feeble stars. The dazzling disk looks as if it were covered with ice or snow

Once again, however, the moon is deceiving us. Despite its apparent brilliance, it is one of the poorest reflectors in the solar system. It sends us only 7 per cent. of the sunlight it receives, and this must be due to the nature of the surface. If the moon had the reflecting power of the cloud-covered planet Venus, the 'evening star' which shines like a lamp in the western sky after the sun has set, it would indeed appear a glorious object.

Obviously, it is important for us to find out as much as we can about the surface structure. Telescopic observations can tell us a great deal about lunar 'geography', and by the time the first space-ship takes off we shall be in a position to provide the travellers with a highly accurate chart of the whole visible disk. On the other hand, we are still rather in the dark about lunar 'geology'. We shall not clear up all the various problems until we can actually examine the surface at close quarters, but recent investigations have given us some information to go on.

Surface temperature

First, what about temperature? Are the explorers likely to experience torrid heat, or bitter cold?

Since the moon sends us light, it is reasonable to assume that it sends us heat as well. If we turn towards the sun, we can feel the hot rays warming us; but the heat sent to us by the moon is so feeble that we cannot possibly feel it on our skins – nor can we record it on an ordinary thermometer. We can, however, measure it by using a large telescope together with a special instrument called a thermocouple, and this was first done by Lord Rosse some seventy years ago.

The principle of the thermocouple is simple enough. If we take two wires made of different metals and make a complete circuit by soldering their ends together, forming a ring, an electric current will flow through the circuit if the joins are at different temperatures. We can therefore produce a current by warming one join and keeping the other at a constant temperature, and this current can be measured with a delicate instrument known as a galvanometer. Rosse concentrated the light (and therefore heat) of the moon on to one join, using his telescope, and measured the strength of the current set up in the circuit. The total heat received could then be worked out.

Some additional corrections had, however, to be made before the proper temperature of the lunar surface could be found A part of the heat received was merely reflected solar heat, the rest, heat which had been absorbed by the lunar surface and then sent out again. Luckily, it did not prove too difficult to separate the wheat from the chaff Owing to its longer wavelength, the genuine surface heat is blocked by a water cell, whereas the reflected solar rays are not; and the amount of heat actually radiated by the warmed surface of the moon can be calculated.

Naturally, Rosse's early results were not very accurate; but they showed that the moon can become very hot indeed, comparable with the temperature of boiling water (212°F.). Recent experiments carried out in America, with highly sensitive thermocouples combined with the world's largest telescopes, have confirmed this. Pettit and Nicholson, working in California with the 100-inch reflector, have calculated that the temperature of the lunar equator rises to 214°F. when the sun is overhead, though it falls to – 58°F. by sunset, and the nights must be bitterly cold--in the region of   250°F., which is about the temperature of liquid air.

These extremes are due to the fact that the moon has almost no atmospheric mantle. It is atmosphere which keeps the surface of a planet at a tolerably level temperature. The uncomfortable conditions resulting from the lack of it are very noticeable upon Mars, where the air is much thinner than on the earth, and even upon the summits of high terrestrial mountains, while every war-time flyer will remember the intense cold at altitudes of 20,000 feet and above The great temperature-range on the moon is going to complicate matters for future colonists, and buildings and space-suits alike will have to be constructed to provide complete protection against both heat and cold.

Moreover, the lunar surface seems to be very bad at holding on to its heat. During an eclipse of the moon, when the solar rays are temporarily cut off, a wave of bitter cold sweeps over the rocks, easily measurable with modern instruments. In 1927, Pettit and Nicholson found that the temperature fell by over 250°F. in about an hour; similar values were found during the eclipse of 1939, so that the surface must be coated with material which has almost no power of keeping warm once the sun has stopped shining on it.

What covers the moon's surface?

This last conclusion has been supported by very recent experiments, made possible by the great developments in radar during the last war Heated bodies send out radiations of all kinds, including the so-called 'radio waves'. In 1949 two Australian investigators, Piddington and Minnett, focused these radio waves into a sensitive receiver by means of a 4-foot metal reflector, and managed to obtain temperature values for the moon by measuring the intensities of the radio waves received. The results were of tremendous interest. The temperatures derived were much more uniform than Pettit and Nicholson's, and it was found that maximum heat did not occur at midday, but three days later. Evidently the outer coating of the moon's surface was more or less transparent to radio waves, so that what Piddington and Minnett were measuring was not the temperature of the sunlit layer, but that of the layers some way under the ground. The time taken for the surface heat to percolate through to the lower layers would account for the delay in reaching peak temperature.

Naturally, the radio waves cannot penetrate far below the surface, and consequently it is evident that the outer covering must be a very poor heat-conductor, protecting the inner layers from the tremendous temperature-range measured with the thermocouple. Well inside the moon, the temperature is constant at about −30°F. (60 degrees below freezing point), which

is considerably above the lowest temperature ever recorded on
the surface of the earth (– 94°F., in Siberia)

Under these circumstances, it may be advisable to transfer at
least some of the early lunar colonies underground. A mole-like
existence has many disadvantages, but would at least mean that
the insulating surface layers could be used as a protection
against extremes of heat and cold, as well as the harmful short-
wave radiations sent out by the sun.

What is this strange covering material, incapable of retaining
heat and almost equally incapable of transmitting the heat
which it receives to the layers below the surface?

We cannot be absolutely certain The light of the moon gives
us little information, because it is merely reflected sunlight; and
the spectroscope, which can split up light from the distant stars
and tell us what elements exist there, is more or less useless.
However, it seems definite that the surface is coated with pul-
verized rock, coarse dust, or some porous material such as
volcanic ash or pumice. On the whole, volcanic ash seems the
most likely answer. The moon has about the right reflecting
power, and its light seems to behave in a suitable fashion; and
as the surface is so obviously volcanic, ash is only to be expected. The nearest terrestrial analogy is perhaps the interior
of Kilauea, in Hawaii. Meteoric dust, too, must be present in
large quantities.

Whether the ash is volcanic or not, it does not form a thick
layer; it is probably not more than a few centimetres in depth,
certainly not more than a few inches. Below it lies the 'true'
surface.

The lunar rocks

If the moon once formed part of the earth, it must be built of
the same material, and the ash-covered rocks are probably
similar to the igneous rocks of the earth. Even if the earth and
moon were never one, it is unlikely that there is a great deal of
difference in the rock structure. Whether we shall find any important minerals which may be used as sources of power, or as
rocket propellents, is another matter. We shall just have to
wait and see.

In 1910 Professor R. W. Wood, of New York, took some

photographs of the moon, using colour plates sensitive to different kinds of light. These led him to believe that a small area not far from the brilliant crater Aristarchus, on the Oceanus Procellarum, was covered with a sulphur deposit, or at any rate something quite unlike the rest of the surface. Sulphur would come as no surprise, as it is another substance intimately associated with volcanoes. In fact, it is so often found around the craters of terrestrial volcanoes that it is still often called 'brimstone', which means 'burning stone'—hence the old religious idea of a 'lake of fire and brimstone'.

Wood's original experiments were made at East Hampton, New York State, with equipment made, as he himself put it, "out of odds and ends" He intended to follow up his investigations, but apparently never did so; and though similar experiments were made eighteen years later by Wright, little further information has been gained.

Is there snow on the moon?

Aristarchus, shown in Plate VIII, presents some special problems. It is by far the brightest spot on the entire moon, and is so glaringly brilliant that it can be made out even when it is on the night side of the moon. Many unwary watchers have mistaken it for an erupting volcano, and it seems probable that even Sir William Herschel, father of stellar astronomy and first President of the Royal Astronomical Society, fell into this trap, though one hesitates to accuse him of it! There must be a definite reason for such strange brightness, which is shared to a lesser degree by Pico, Menelaus in the Hæmus Mountains, Proclus near the Mare Crisium, and a number of other formations.

W. H. Pickering, author of the famous photographic atlas of 1904, attributed it to snow. He believed that cracks in the lunar surface sent out water vapour, which was at once re-deposited as snow, and became conspicuous because of its greater reflecting power; but there are any number of serious difficulties in the way of this idea.

For one thing, mountain-tops are the very last places where we should expect to find snow on the moon. It would be far more likely to hide itself in the shadowed valleys and gorges.

Moreover, the fierce heat of the lunar day would seem to rule out the possibility -particularly as Aristarchus and its kind are at their most brilliant under high light; and can we seriously believe in snow and water vapour upon a world where there is no moisture and virtually no air, where the daytime temperature is scalding hot and the surface is coated with the ash of dead and dying volcanoes? It does not seem reasonable, and we must reluctantly look for another explanation.

The brilliance of Aristarchus and similar formations must be due to some difference in their surface ash, which reflects more strongly than the usual type. The ash forming the rays may well be similar, and it is noticeable that ray-craters are usually bright-walled. Tycho, for instance, is extremely luminous under a high sun. Many of the smaller objects which are either bright-walled or surrounded by bright areas are themselves centres of minor ray systems; a particularly good example is Euclides, close to the Riphæn Mountains, which is surrounded by a luminous nimbus and also sends out a few short rays.

Colour on the moon

A world like the moon, barren, arid and bleak, naturally lacks colour. There are no vivid blues, greens or reds anywhere —only the black shadows and the various shades of ash-grey. From time to time definite hues are reported, but all are faint and fugitive.

It is true that the Maria are not identical in colour. The pure grey of the Mare Imbrium contrasts with the lighter patchiness of the Mare Nubium, and both the Mare Crisium and the Palus Somnii are said to be greenish, while the Mare Frigoris is reputedly a dirty yellow. These latter colours are not at all conspicuous, however, and the writer has never seen them.

Now and then we come across something more definite. Between 1830 and 1838, Mädler frequently recorded a reddish patch near the little crater Lichtenberg, which lies between Aristarchus and the limb. This tint was not seen again for more than a century, but then Barcroft reobserved it, describing it as "a pronounced reddish-brown or orange colour around the craterlet". This was followed in 1951 by an interesting observation made by R. M. Baum, in England, who recorded a short-lived ruddy glow lasting for less than half an hour. Undoubtedly Baum's glow was due to the solar rays falling at a particular angle on some unusual surface deposit, and this must also be the explanation of the colour seen by Mädler and Barcroft.

Other colours have been reported from time to time -Aristarchus, for instance, has been said to show bluish patches on its wall but the eye is easily deceived, and the startling colours periodically reported by observers with small telescopes must invariably be put down to optical defects in their eyes or instruments.

The lack of colour is only one of the many ways in which the lunar landscape will seem strange to the first explorers. The conditions will be 'unearthly', in every sense of the word. For instance, we shall feel remarkably light- because the moon's gravitational pull is much weaker than the earth's and a violent leap will carry us up 20 or 30 feet. Neither shall we be able to talk normally. Sound-waves are carried by air, and on the nearly airless moon there is eternal silence. Still, we have a good idea of what to expect; and it is now time for us to anticipate the future by transporting ourselves, in imagination, to some of the places which will be explored by men of the twenty-first century.

CHAPTER 8

LUNAR LANDSCAPES

ONE advantage of 'touring in imagination' is that we can cover vast distances. It will be time enough to worry about transport when we travel to the moon in reality, not only in thought; and for the moment we are bound by no restrictions either in space or time. We have landed, as the first rocket probably will land, in the great Ocean of Storms, so let us leave our space-craft and make our way to the starting-point of our journey, the bottom of the great Herodotus cleft-valley (Plates VIII, IX). The sun is just setting on the outer plain, but it is of no help to us within the valley. No gleams of solar light can reach us, and the heavens above are black and star-studded.

The lunar sky

Our first thought is that the darkness seems far more intense than anything in our earthly experience. On our own planet, it is seldom really 'dark'. During summer, it is twilight in England for most of the night; and even in midwinter there is usually a certain amount of glow from overhead, even when there is a thick mantle of cloud This is not the case on the moon, where there is no air to diffuse the light. The earth, of course, shines brilliantly, but we cannot see it from the bottom of our valley, and the blackness would be absolute but for the stars above.

It is bitterly cold, too. We are of course wearing protective suits–otherwise we could not possibly survive for a moment, partly because of the lack of pressure and partly because the temperature is in the region of $-250°F.$, cold enough to liquefy ordinary air. There is no atmosphere to diffuse the sun's heat, and the insulating surface layers allow little or no warmth to percolate through the ground.

Let us take a more careful look at the stars. We are in an excellent position to observe them, on the upper plain they could not at present be seen nearly so well. It has often been said that the sun and the stars could be seen simultaneously from the moon, as the lunar sky is black and not blue; but this idea is not correct, owing to the glare from the sunlit rocks. However, the inner walls of our valley are in full shadow, and there is nothing to prevent us from seeing the stars above in their full glory.

We notice immediately that they are not twinkling. Twinkling is another atmospheric effect, so that it does not occur on the airless moon. The stars shine down as hard, steely points of light, quite unlike the gently winking orbs of terrestrial skies. Moreover, there seem to be a great many of them Astronomically, the earth's atmospheric blanket is a great handicap to observation, and now that we are free of it we can see much more clearly.

The next unfamiliar fact is that the stars seem to be moving extremely slowly. The earth turns on its axis once every twenty-four hours, so that a star on the celestial equator takes only twelve hours to move right across the sky from horizon to horizon, but on the slower-spinning moon the corresponding time is a fortnight. We shall be able to gauge this later by watching the progress of sunrise. There is no friendly dawn; the first rays appear over the horizon without the slightest warning, stabbing the jet-black heavens, but it takes more than an hour for the complete disk of the sun to rise above the skyline.

Our Pole Star, too, is not the pole star of the moon. The lunar celestial pole moves more quickly than ours, and describes a small circle in the sky once every eighteen years; the nearest bright star to its average position is a rather inadequate one named Zeta Draconis—about as bright as the faintest of the seven stars in the Great Bear As the latitude of the Herodotus valley is about 20°N., the celestial pole is not high above the horizon, and at the moment it is hidden by the rocky walls of the cleft.

In the valley

There are many other unfamiliar things about the sky, but it is time to turn our attention to the valley itself Our electric torches show us that although the rocks are deathly cold, they are not damp, as is the case in terrestrial caves such as the Cheddar tunnels or the Grottos of Han. We forget that damp-ness means water, and there is no water anywhere on the moon.

F

Nor are the walls of the valley sheer. They are certainly steep, but with our bodies lightened by the moon's lesser gravitational pull we ought to be able to climb them without a great deal of difficulty.

If we grope westwards along the valley, we shall find ourselves turning towards the south, while the gorge becomes less deep and finally opens out into the curious formation known as the Cobra-Head. This is obviously an old crater, as it is more or less circular and even has a low mound to represent a central mountain; and from it narrower, steeper branches lead on to the floor of the large walled plain Herodotus. There is also a branch leading north-east, and this is the one for us to follow.

It, too, is of considerable depth, and though it is comparatively narrow the walls are even steeper than those of the valley we have just left. It seems to be almost straight, and in the pitch-darkness there is little to be seen. We are in for a long walk; but after 40 miles or more we come to a junction, and find that we have arrived back in the main valley, which winds eastwards across the plain until it finally ends in a small craterlet.

The shining earth

We have not seen much of the moon as yet, and we still have to obtain our first view of the earth. For this we must climb out of the valley on to the outer surface, and we shall do well to make for the small crater Bruce, in the Sinus Medii or Central Bay, close to the centre of the moon's apparent disk. To get there, we have to travel across the Oceanus Procellarum and the northernmost part of the Mare Nubium, passing not far from the majestic crater-ring of Copernicus and the ancient, wrecked Stadius. The sun has set now, and the landscape is plunged in the depths of lunar night, so that it is an eerie journey among the ghostly, silent craters of the lonely plain. By the time we reach Bruce, it is lunar midnight. This means that it is new moon on the earth, and consequently full earth on the moon; our home-planet looks a truly magnificent orb, flooding the rocks with light and shining down from overhead with a splendid, glowing radiance.

Even with the unaided eye we can make out considerable detail on the disk, which is twelve times the size that the moon appears from the earth. Continents and seas are plain enough – the Americas can be seen easily, and also the bluish area marking the Pacific Ocean – and the polar areas, which Scott, Amundsen and many other pioneers risked their lives to explore, are mantled in white. We can see, too, that there is a blanket of air round the disk, as the edge does not appear hard and sharp, but surrounded by a luminous aureole far more splendid than the most magnificent solar halo.

As we watch, we see changes. The stars move slowly – very slowly; it takes them an hour to shift as much as they do in two minutes seen from the earth – but the earth stays quite still in the heavens, although its axial spinning is revealed by the drift of the continents and seas from left to right. The Americas pass from view over the limb, and presently Africa and Europe can be made out; with our binoculars we can even distinguish tiny England, appearing very unimportant from a distance of a quarter of a million miles, and not very far from the limits of the northern ice-cap. Now and then the slow drift of a star takes it behind the earth, but we find it difficult to see the actual disappearance, as the star becomes drowned in the glowing ring of light caused by the terrestrial atmosphere.

We shall have to wait for some time if we want to see any marked change in the earth's phase, so let us look more closely at our surroundings – we can see them quite well by the earth-light. The crater in which we stand, Bruce, is neither large nor deep. It is about 6 miles across, with walls rising to perhaps 1,000 feet above the floor, and if we walk to the middle of it we shall find it hard to realize that we are inside a crater at all. It is much more like a flat dish. The ramparts slope gently up to their crests, and we have no difficulty in scaling them, only to find that even on their summits we are not far above the outer level of the Central Bay. Here and there are mounds, and everywhere we see tiny craterlets and pits, while in the distance a mountain-top gleams in the earth-light.

Where the sun never sets

It will take a week for 'full earth' to wane to 'half earth', and rather than wait for it let us leave Bruce and go to a very different region, that of the so-called 'Mountains of Eternal

Light'. They are a long way off–we have to cross the Mare Vaporum, the Hæmus Mountains, and the comparatively level Mare Serenitatis, passing round the western foothills of the Caucasus range. The Mountains of Eternal Light are close to the North Pole, and the nearest formation marked on the outline map is Shackleton, right on the limb, a walled plain over 50 miles across (large enough to hold Sussex and Surrey put together), broken in the south-east by a smaller, deeper plain named Gioja. Shackleton has broken into an even more damaged plain about equal to it in size, and which actually contains the Pole. Our mountains are on the far side of this, and as we are some 10,000 feet above the general surface level we have a good view of the surrounding terrain.

We are in full sunlight - because the mountains, placed as they are, are always in sunlight. The sun never sets on their summits, and night is unknown. Around us loom the tangled masses of peaks and the gorge-entrances; low down in the sky we can see the earth, gibbous now, and almost touching the tumbled rocks that make up the horizon. Below, we look down into the shadows The rays which catch our peak pass over the lower-lying valleys, and we seem to be cut off from the rest of the moon, in a universe of our own.

It is only in the regions known as the 'libration zones', round the edge of the earth-turned hemisphere, that the earth appears to rise and set. The earth is not absolutely stationary in the lunar sky. The libration effects make it sway slightly to and fro. From the equatorial and mid-latitude zones of the moon, the earth's swaying is not noticeable; near the poles, where we can use the horizon for reference, it is obvious enough, and right at the edge of the earth-turned hemisphere the librational swaying takes the earth alternately just above and just below the horizon. From the 'hidden hemisphere' of the moon, the earth cannot, of course, be seen at all.

The great crater Pythagoras

Some 350 miles east of the Pole lies Pythagoras, a tremendous walled plain which is certainly worth a visit, even though we shall have to cross some very rough country to get there. Travelling in time as well as in space, we arrive just after the sun has

risen once more above the horizon, to find that Pythagoras'
inner east wall is fully lit by the comforting solar rays. There is
a central elevation, too—a massive mountain rising to 5,000 feet
above the floor, though it slopes fairly gently and we have no
difficulty in scaling it. We find that the top does not rise to a
sharp crest, but is broad and without any one main summit; and
near its centre we find something strangely reminiscent of an
earthly volcano—a 'hill-top' crater, with a rim rising only slightly
above the level of the surrounding rocks, and a saucer-like
interior. It is not the highest point of the mountain mass, as
there is a peak to the east of it, but as it is a full mile in diameter
it is quite conspicuous, and it will take us some time to walk
across it.

We cross the top of the low rim, and walk down into the
crater itself. There is no need to scramble, though now and then
we have to jump a dozen feet or so over tangled rocks, and the
surface is never level. When we are right inside, it is clear enough
that we are standing in a circular depression, even though the
walls are low and higher peaks can be seen beyond them.

We shall have a better view if we scale the summit on the far
side of the crater, and this we can easily do. We are now at the
highest point of the mountain, and can look down into the
formation itself, but at first sight we are rather disappointed.

We know that Pythagoras is 85 miles in diameter, with walls
17,000 feet above its floor, but there seems nothing cavernous or
precipitous about it from where we stand. The central mountain
slopes gently down to the floor in a mass of ashy, broken rocks
and débris; two other mountain-masses, almost as high as ours,
can be seen to the south-west, catching the rays of the rising
sun; but the main eastern walls, lofty though they really are,
appear very inconspicuous and low down on the horizon. We
do not seem to be inside a walled plain at all.

The explanation is quite simple. The moon is much smaller
than the earth, and its surface curves much more sharply, so
that the horizon is much nearer. If we stood on a perfectly
regular plain (supposing that such a thing existed on the moon),
the horizon would only be just over 2 miles away from us.

Ptolemæus

We have now been on the moon for well over a fortnight, and even though we are travelling only in imagination it is time we had rest and food. Our space-craft is waiting for us, but our meal is rather unappetizing. No edible plants can grow on the barren lunar surface, and everything has to be brought from earth, so that we have to put up with a diet of concentrates. We are content to leave the choice of our next observation-point to our pilot; and when we wake, we find that we have arrived at a plain which we know must be near the centre of our outline map, as the earth is high in the sky--no longer full, but a crescent. The sun, too, is high above the horizon, shining down with a hard whitish glare untempered by any shielding atmosphere. The surface where we stand appears to be rather darker in hue than that near Pythagoras, and there are no lofty hills anywhere around.

Some way away we can see a low rim which turns out to belong to a crater 5 miles in diameter, with a bowl-shaped interior and gently sloping walls; and there are any number of low mounds and ridges, together with saucer-like depressions so shallow that it is difficult for us to tell whether we are in one or not. It comes as a surprise to learn that the 5-mile crater is Lyot, and that we are standing right in the amphitheatre of the great walled plain known as Ptolemæus.

From the earth, Ptolemæus looks like a distinct hollow. Certainly its walls, broken and breached though they are, do contain peaks thousands of feet above the floor; but from our present position we are unable to see any of them--the horizon is too close. Even if we walk the 30 miles to the north-western border of Ptolemæus, we shall be able to reach the outer country without doing any mountaineering. There are broad valleys separating the sections of the broken rampart, and we may not realize at first that we are passing through the border at all. Still, we shall notice a difference in the character of the landscape, as the floor of Ptolemæus is much smoother than the rough surface outside.

Mount Argæus

As the sun slowly climbs through the inky sky, and the shadows shorten, we make our way north-westwards, past the ruined plain Hipparchus (majestic from the earth, very obscure when seen close at hand), past the twin craters Godin and Agrippa, and across the comparatively level eastern part of the great Mare Tranquillitatis. The lunar morning is as long as a terrestrial week, and as we travel we watch the crescent earth gradually narrowing. By 'midday' we have reached our goal— Mount Argæus, on the western side of the broad strait which separates the Sea of Tranquillity from its eastern neighbour, the Sea of Serenity.

This time we really do have some impression of height. Even from earth we can see that Argæus is fairly steep, as it casts a long, tapering shadow when the sun is low over it; and as we look down the slope leading to the strait, 8,000 feet below, we have a splendid view.

Argæus itself is not a single peak It is a mountain mass, roughly triangular in shape and threaded with ravines and gullies. Although the slopes are steep, particularly towards the strait, they are by no means precipitous except for short stretches here and there; but the sharpness of the rocks, untempered by erosion, is very noticeable.

The strait itself is comparatively level. We can make out the rim of a shallow crater, and the usual small pits and mounds; and there is also a deep, narrow cleft, starting at the foot of Argæus and running south-east. To the west, the slope is gentler and the surface rougher, though we are standing on the highest point for a long way around. Across the strait, over 100 miles away and far beyond the horizon, lies Cape Acherusia, another rocky promontory half the height of Argæus and marking the western end of the Hæmus mountain chain; and slightly north of this, Plinius, the 'sentinel crater' guarding the entrance to the Mare Serenitatis.

The Washbowl

Next let us visit the Washbowl,[1] which can almost be classed

---

[1] This curious object was given its most appropriate name by Dr Wilkins, when he and the writer observed it through the great telescope at the Observatory of Meudon. It had not previously been recorded except as a simple peak

as another lunar freak. It is to be found inside the crater Cassini, a formation with low, narrow walls, lying in the Mare Imbrium near the foothills of the Alps. To reach it, we shall have to pass from Argæus right across the Mare Serenitatis, crossing the serpentine ridge and perhaps pausing to examine the much-discussed Linné, and go through the strait separating the Apennines from the Caucasus. This strait is not nearly so level as that between Argæus and Acherusia. It is littered with hummocks, mounds and rocky débris, with clefts and mountain masses here and there, and altogether it is extremely rough. Walking would be easy enough, in view of our new-found ability to spring 20 feet from the ground; but the walk from Argæus to the Washbowl would be a long one. If we could drive a car across the Mare Serenitatis at a steady 60 m.p.h. it would take us seven hours to get from one side to the other.

Passing by Thætetus, the crater described earlier on, we come at last to the ramparts of Cassini, which do not rise much above the level of the plain. Moreover, the 'glacis', or outer slope, is very long and gentle, so that we have to spend some time in climbing it. At last we are inside Cassini, and after a further 10 miles' travel across the relatively smooth floor we come to a smaller crater, Cassini A, 11 miles across. It is inside A that we finally find the Washbowl.

From the earth, the Washbowl looks very like a peak; but as we climb up we find that it is really a shallow crater, with massive rounded walls, and a minute central orifice only a few hundred yards across. We can walk across the whole Bowl in half an hour, and if the rounded ramparts did not gleam white in the sunlight they would be hard to make out from the earth. To the south-west, the level of the plain drops before rising again to the distant ramparts of Cassini A beyond the horizon; there is no such drop to the north, and we realize that inside Cassini A, with its northern boundary marked by the Washbowl, is a very old ring. Now that we examine the area more critically, we can detect hills and hummocks which seem to mark the site of an old wall, and 4 or 5 miles to the east we can see the top of a peak, perhaps as high as Shropshire's Wrekin.

Across the Apennines

From the Washbowl we travel south-west, past Thætetus once more and up towards the foothills of the mighty Apennines. The country grows steadily rougher and rougher, and at last the tops of great mountains appear over the horizon. We see Mount Hadley towering 15,000 feet into the sky, which is still jet-black even though the sun is well above the horizon and the rock-glare hides the stars; and gradually the mountains close in upon us, until all we can see is a tumbled, broken mass in every direction, with here and there a giant peak Each time we move into shadow, we pass from glaring sunlight into absolute blackness; and in the shade, where the solar rays are cut off, the cold is so bitter that to expose ourselves to it for the fraction of a second would mean death.

At last, when we are far above the plain behind us and completely hemmed in by the rocks, we stumble towards the rim of a bright little formation, Aratus 6 miles across, with a sunken floor and a wall that seems to be almost level with the rocks outside. Its bowl-shaped interior contains the usual pits and mounds, and from the inside our view is very much restricted. To either side there are lowering mountains, throwing long, icy shadows across us. Gradually, with the slow, stately march of all the heavenly bodies as seen from the moon- the earth, now visible once more as a slender crescent, excepted—the sun sinks behind a peak, and the shadows lengthen until the little crater is enveloped in the bitter cold of a lunar evening.

The Straight Wall

Our last visit is perhaps the most interesting of all. We are to go to the Straight Wall in the Mare Nubium, well south of the equator. As the sun sets on Aratus, we leave it to the desolation of night, and make our way back through the valleys of the Apennines on to the plain below.

The Straight Wall is a long way off. To get there, we can either break back through the Apennines, cross the Mare Vaporum, pass by Bruce in the Sinus Medii and come up the western coast of the Mare Nubium past Ptolemæus, or skirt the Apennines on their eastern side, go through the strait separating

Eratosthenes from the Carpathian Mountains, pass by the ruins of old Stadius, and cross the comparatively flat plain near the lava-damaged Fra Mauro. Whichever way we choose, we come at last to the great fault, and find a spectacle that is more than worth the quarter-million-mile journey from the earth to the moon.

The so-called Wall is really a tremendous cliff. It is 60 miles long, so that it would stretch from London to Winchester, and ends to the south in a cluster of hills known as the Stag's-Horn Mountains. The plain to the east drops suddenly by over 800 feet, exposing a line of steep cliffs which gleam in the evening sunlight as we approach. Here, for once, we have a really towering rock-face, as steep as the Palisades of the Hudson River, and find that it is still fiercely hot, although the general surface temperature has fallen to below freezing-point now that the sun is about to set. The vertical cliff-face faces the sun, and still receives the rays full on it instead of at a low angle; and this accounts for it being so much hotter than the rest of the ground.

As we have come from the north, we have arrived at the loftiest part of the Wall, and from the surface of the Mare Nubium we gaze in wonder at the cliffs rising above us. They become slightly less lofty as we make our way southwards, but there is plenty to see. Presently we come to twin craterlets, both very shallow, and some miles to the east we can make out the ramparts of Birt, a crater 11 miles across. Birt's walls are rather unusually elevated above the Mare surface, but even so they do not appear lofty from our position at the foot of the Straight Wall, because the horizon is so near. At last we come to the first of the Stag's-Horn peaks, and it will pay us to thread our way through them, round the southern end of the great fault, and approach the Wall from the west.

The aspect is very different. The plain has much the same character as before it is a little rougher, if anything but the Wall itself is not to be seen. East of us lies what looks like a low ridge, and on climbing it we solve the mystery, for below us, dropping steeply away, is the familiar cliff. Far below is the plain, studded here and there with pits and craterlets which cast long shadows as the sun sinks down to the horizon, touching it with its disk and almost imperceptibly passing out of sight.

Our imaginary journey is over. Perhaps, before very long, we shall be able to do away with imagination, and see these wonders for ourselves; but meanwhile let us take a final look at the grey plain, as the last rays of the sun shine over the horizon and catch the face of the gaunt, glittering cliff, before the icy chill of lunar night overtakes it and plunges it into a darkness relieved only by the cold, steely stars and the comforting light of the glowing earth.

CHAPTER 9

THE LUNAR ATMOSPHERE

OUR wanderings upon the lunar surface have shown us that the moon is even less like the earth than we had supposed. Generally speaking, however, we can trace most of the differences back to one fundamental thing–the lack of air. It is this which causes the silence, the dryness, the blackness of the sky, the ruggedness of the scenery and the violent extremes of temperature; and because of it, we shall never be able to walk about unprotected. This is also why it will be necessary for even the early colonists to build great airtight domes.

Why is the moon almost airless?

Despite the statements so often met with in textbooks, there is a little air left on the moon. However, the atmosphere is extremely thin, and no earth-born creature could possibly breathe it. If the moon was once part of the earth, it is reasonable to assume that it took its fair share of atmosphere with it when it broke away;[1] so what has turned it into the almost airless planet that it now is?

The answer is that the moon is less massive than the earth, and so does not pull so strongly. Every body, large or small, has a certain amount of gravitational attraction, and the more massive the body the stronger the pull. The sun, well over 300,000 times as massive as the earth, pulls so strongly that it rules the entire solar system, and holds the planets in a vice-like grip; on the other hand tiny worlds, such as the smaller asteroids and the two satellites of Mars, pull very feebly. A man who jumped up from the surface of Deimos, the smaller and more distant of the two Martian moons, would never come down–as the attraction of Deimos would not be strong enough to hold him–and he would sail off into interplanetary space.

It may help us to appreciate this if we compare the sun and

---

[1] Of course, the moon may never have been part of the earth, as was pointed out in Chapter 3

Deimos to two magnets, one immensely powerful and the other very weak–though it must be borne in mind that the force of gravity has nothing to do with magnetic force. If we coat our two magnets with iron filings, and shake them violently, the filings will not stir from the surface of the 'sun', but will fall away from the feeble magnet representing Deimos. The earth comes about midway between these two extremes.

If I hold a cricket-ball in my hand, and drop it, it falls to the ground, because it is pulled by the earth's gravitational attraction. It is equally true to say that the cricket-ball is trying to pull the earth up to meet it, but the mass of the earth is so tremendous, compared to that of the ball, that it is the ball which is the more affected; the movement of the earth is far too minute to be noticed.

If I throw the ball into the air, it will rise to some distance, slackening in speed as it goes, and then pause and fall back to the ground. The harder I throw it, the higher it will rise before losing all its initial speed, and the longer it will take to fall back into my hands.

If I have enough strength to hurl the ball upwards at a speed of seven miles a second, I shall wait in vain for it to fall back. The ball has been given such a tremendous starting-speed that even the massive earth has not been able to hold it down, and it has shot away into space, never to return. This critical speed of seven miles a second is known as the earth's 'velocity of escape'.[1]

The velocity of escape on tiny Deimos is not nearly so high. It would be quite unnecessary to throw the ball at seven miles a second, and, as we have seen, it would be possible to jump clear of the satellite altogether. Even on the moon, the critical speed is only one and a half miles a second, and it is because of this low escape velocity that there is so little air.

Air is made up of molecules, which are themselves made up of groups of atoms. A molecule is almost unbelievably small, and instead of giving any actual figures–which would be meaningless, as they are too large to appreciate–it will be better to

[1] Air-resistance has not been taken into account in this description, as it makes no difference to the general principle. However, it would be rather difficult to throw a cricket-ball at 7 miles a second. This can be judged from the fact that Lindwall bowls at something like 1/40 of a mile a second!

give an example. Take a small box with a capacity of 1 cubic inch, and fill it with ordinary air. If we release 10 million molecules every second, how long will it take the box to empty itself completely? A second a minute a month? No; 50 million years! Our brains are quite unable to take in anything so tiny, and obviously we have no hope of seeing an independent molecule even with a powerful microscope.

However, everything–however small- is subject to gravity, and the molecules of the earth's atmosphere are no exception. They move about at high speeds, and some kinds of molecules move faster than others. The lighter the molecule, the greater its speed, and the molecules of hydrogen, the lightest of the gases, are particularly fast-moving.

If a molecule can work up to a speed greater than the velocity of escape, it may break free from the earth's attraction altogether and travel away into space. So far as hydrogen is concerned, this is not difficult A series of collisions with its companions can increase the speed of a hydrogen molecule well beyond the limit, and so all the free hydrogen originally present in the atmosphere has leaked away. Oxygen and nitrogen, which make up most of our present atmosphere, are heavier and slower-moving, so that the earth has been able to hold them down; and carbon dioxide, or carbonic acid gas, the gas found in ordinary soda-water, is heavier still

The moon, with its reduced velocity of escape, is much less effective at holding down its molecules; and not only the hydrogen but nearly everything else as well has leaked away. What is left must be made up of relatively heavy, slow molecules, and oxygen is definitely absent; so that even if the lunar atmosphere turned out to be thousands of times denser than is believed to be the case, we should still be unable to breathe it.

The air of other worlds

To make the position perfectly clear, it will be worth while spending a few moments in considering the atmospheres of other worlds in the solar system. Jupiter, the giant planet, has an escape velocity of 38 miles a second. Consequently, it has kept all its original hydrogen, and this has combined with other elements to form an atmosphere made up largely of two evil-smelling hydrogen compounds, ammonia and methane. The smell of ammonia is well known, and methane is the pungent explosive gas known to miners as the dreaded 'fire-damp', so that any visitors to Jupiter would have to provide themselves with something very special in the way of gas-masks –though it is certain enough that even in the remote future, when travel between the inner planets is an accomplished fact, it will be out of the question to attempt a landing on the gas-hidden surface of Jupiter.

Saturn, Uranus and Neptune are similar, and of more interest to us is Titan, sixth satellite of Saturn, which has almost twice the mass of the moon, and an escape velocity of 2 miles a second. There is definitely an atmosphere here, though it seems to be composed principally of methane and is certainly un-breathable.

Mars, the Red Planet, with an escape velocity of three and a quarter miles a second, has an atmosphere made up chiefly of nitrogen, with a measurable amount of carbon dioxide but very little oxygen; and tiny worlds such as the asteroids and the two Martian satellites have lost every vestige of air.

Thinness of the lunar atmosphere

It is quite obvious that the moon does not possess an atmosphere in any way comparable to the earth's. For one thing, the lunar limb appears hard and sharp. If surrounded by an air-blanket, it would show a luminous aureole –as the earth actually does, seen from the moon. When the moon passes in front of the sun, during a solar eclipse, the limb is still perfectly hard and clear-cut, and no trace of any atmospheric absorption has ever been observed.

Better evidence still is afforded by occultations of stars. An occultation takes place when the moon appears to pass in front of a star, and this often happens; when the moon passes through a star-cluster such as the Pleiades (the Seven Sisters), half a dozen naked-eye stars may be occulted within a few hours. In each case the star will be seen to shine steadily right up to the disk, and then snap out like a candle-flame in the wind, as the limb passes over it. There is no flickering, no wavering in its light until the moment of disappearance.

An occultation of a brilliant star at the moon's dark limb is an impressive spectacle. Unless lit by earthshine, the dark limb is naturally invisible, and the star seems suddenly blotted from view as though a mighty dark hand has swept across it. The reappearance at the bright limb, some time later, is equally startling. One moment, the star is not there; the next, it is shining against the limb with full brilliance.

Stellar occultations provide us with something more definite than the mere fact that a star seems to snap out without flickering beforehand. If a belt of air existed round the lunar limb, it should bend or 'refract' the light-rays coming from the star, just before the star itself passes behind the moon (we can see an example of refraction when we shine a torch into a tank of water; the beam is obviously bent), and the effect of this would be to keep the star in view for a little longer than would otherwise be the case.[1] If we predict the time of occultation, and then observe the actual time of disappearance, there should be a difference, if the lunar air is dense enough to produce any appreciable degree of refraction; and the amount of the difference ought to give a key to the density of the atmosphere responsible for it.

Unfortunately, the results of experiments made along these lines are hopelessly discordant. The trouble is that the lunar limb is very rough. If the star passes behind a mountain, it will naturally vanish sooner than if it passes behind a valley. The difference is quite unimportant in the ordinary way; but when we are considering intervals of much less than a second, it is quite enough to wreck the accuracy of the method completely. We simply cannot predict the occultations accurately enough. Sir George Airy, who was Astronomer Royal from 1835 to 1881, believed that there were indications of definite refraction; but later observations do not confirm this, and we must look elsewhere for proofs of an atmosphere.

Professor W. H. Pickering, one of the greatest American

---

[1] It is actually possible to see both the sun and the moon before they really rise, as refraction lifts them into view when they are still completely below the horizon. On several occasions, the sun and the full moon have been seen simultaneously, just above opposite horizons When the sun or moon is rising, the bottom part of the disk is more affected by refraction than the top, and this is why the disk often appears flattened.

planetary observers of the past century, turned to occultations of the planets. Planets, like stars, may be occulted; but as a planet shows a disk, and does not appear as a mere point, the disappearance is gradual It takes some seconds for the lunar limb to glide across the planet, cutting it off from view.

As Jupiter passed behind the moon, in 1892, Pickering observed a dark band crossing the planet's disk, tilted with respect to the well-known surface belts. This he attributed to the absorbing effect of a lunar atmosphere. The observation was repeated at several other occultations, and it was noted that the dark band only appeared when the planet was cut by the moon's bright limb; at the dark or 'night' limb of the moon it was not seen, and Pickering concluded from this that the lunar atmosphere responsible for it was frozen solid during the lunar night. The band was also recorded by two of Pickering's colleagues, Barnard and Douglass

Pickering then worked out the probable density of the lunar atmosphere, and announced that the surface density was about 1/1,800 as great as that of the earth's atmosphere at sea-level. Unfortunately, however, more recent investigations have proved that the true density cannot be anything like as great as this. 1/10,000 of the terrestrial sea-level density is the maximum possible value which can be accepted, and this is so much less than Pickering's estimate that we are bound to question whether much reliance can be placed upon his investigations. Moreover, the dark band has not been confirmed at later occultations - and the human eye is very easily deceived.

If there is any atmosphere around the moon, it ought to produce a faint twilight effect. An English astronomer, Russell, searched unsuccessfully for it in 1926, and the photographic search carried out in 1949 by two French observers, Lyot and Dollfus, was also negative. Lyot and Dollfus were working at the Pic du Midi, the loftiest observatory in the world, which is built on the top of a peak in the Pyrenees above the densest layers of the earth's atmosphere, so that they enjoyed very favourable conditions; and they concluded that the ground density of the lunar air was certainly less than 1/10,000 of ours.

Two Russian investigators, Fesenkov and Lipski, attacked the problem in a different way. If there is a lunar atmosphere,

G

it must cause a 'twilight effect' on the non-sunlit hemisphere of the moon, and the 'twilight' would be rather different from ordinary light; special instruments should be able to work out which was which. The original experiments, made by Fesenkov in 1943, revealed nothing definite; but Lipski, in 1949, believed that he had definitely found an atmosphere with a ground-density of 1/10,000 of ours.[1] This result has not yet been confirmed, and more evidence is necessary before we can accept it; but at least we have something to go on.

All these theoretical investigations seem to lead us back to an atmosphere with a ground-density of something like 1/10,000 of our own. This is far less than that at the top of Mount Everest, and indeed corresponds to what we normally call a laboratory vacuum, so that even if it was made of pure oxygen no earth-creature would be able to breathe it. However, thin though it is, it is likely to prove of the greatest importance; and the best proofs of its existence are to be obtained by direct observations, made at the eye-end of a telescope.

Twilight on the moon

First, let us go back to lunar twilight. Despite Lyot and Dollfus' failure to detect it, what appears to be definite indications of twilight at the horns of the crescent moon has often been recorded. It was first seen by Schröter, who frequently recorded the horns prolonged in a luminous ring along the dark side of the moon, and regarded the appearance as certain proof of an atmosphere. Unfortunately, Schröter's estimate of the air-density – 1/30 of the earth's – was obviously very wide of the mark, and there can be no doubt that he was only too anxious to believe in a reasonably dense atmosphere around a world which he thought to be living and changing. Schröter's honesty cannot be doubted, but this time it is certain that he was misled.

However, similar appearances have been recorded by dozens of other observers. Even Mädler, who was so firmly convinced that the moon is a dead world, saw them; and he and Beer con-

---

[1] Dollfus, at the Pic, has recently detected an atmosphere on the planet Mercury by this method, and states that its density is about 1/350 of ours, corresponding to a barometric pressure of about 1 mm Hg Mercury's escape velocity, however, is 2½ miles a second, appreciably greater than the moon's

cluded that it was impossible to doubt the existence of a tenuous atmosphere. There is no point in listing many of the particular observations, but one or two may be mentioned as typical of all the rest. On March 20 1912, W. S Franks, using a good 6-inch refracting telescope at East Grinstead, in Sussex, saw the south horn prolonged along the Leibnitz Mountains as a feeble line of light well into the dark hemisphere; on April 14 1948, Dr Wilkins saw the star-like points of light caused by mountain-tops catching the solar rays, joined by feeble filaments of light much brighter than the earthshine. Similar appearances have been seen in recent years by numerous observers, including Professor W. H. Haas and D. P. Barcroft, of the Association of Lunar and Planetary Observers, and the present writer. There can be no doubt that the phenomenon is a genuine one, and not due to any trick of the light.

The trouble with most of these twilight observations is that it is not easy to disentangle true twilight from earthshine. The earthshine, known popularly as "the Old Moon in the Young Moon's arms", is generally to be seen during the crescent phase, when the light reflected from our own world is strong enough to make the night hemisphere of the moon faintly luminous. Moreover, earthlight behaves in much the same way that twilight would do, and this is why Lipski's reported discovery of a definite lunar atmosphere by this method must be regarded with a certain amount of reserve.

Neither is it quite clear why twilight effects are only seen occasionally, and not at every crescent moon. It is probable that the tenuous lunar 'air' does freeze during the bitterly cold nights though as we have no definite knowledge of its composition, we cannot be sure about this—and the twilight at the horns may therefore be due to the vaporizing of the frozen gas as the sun rises upon it.

If the amount of atmosphere deposited in the solid form is not exactly the same at each place each night, the observed twilights may mark slight local condensations where, by chance, more has been deposited than usual. Of course, this is pure speculation; but it is worth noting that carbon dioxide, which, as we shall see later, may well make up most of the lunar atmosphere, solidifies very easily.

Mists on the moon

Apart from twilight effects, well-defined mists have been seen
on the moon from time to time. They are very slight, and in no
way comparable to terrestrial fogs -they certainly do not con-
sist of water vapour–but they appear occasionally, and their
reality cannot be questioned.

There are many records of mists inside 'the Greater Black
Lake', Plato, the dark-floored crater on the borders of the Mare
Imbrium, and obscurations undoubtedly take place on the floor.
In a small telescope the interior appears dark, uniform grey;
with larger instruments, some tiny craterlets and white spots
appear, but the various maps and charts made of them during
the last seventy years do not agree at all well. Some details often
recorded as 'conspicuous' are unaccountably missed at other
times, while previously faint objects show up well. There are
also cases of the floor appearing totally blank under good conditions, with telescopes which should certainly have shown a
considerable amount of detail. The only satisfactory answer to
the puzzle is that mists occur on the floor, hiding the small
features beneath an opaque haze.

One particular example may be cited. Under Plato's eastern
wall, A. S. Williams recorded a white spot in 1892. Birt, who
had paid great attention to Plato, had drawn a chart sixteen
years before, and had not shown it. To Dr. Steavenson, in 1920,
it appeared as a definite crater with inner shadow, and one of
the more conspicuous features of the floor. The telescope used
was the 28-inch refractor at Greenwich Observatory, and the
craterlet was recorded on several occasions. Yet to Dr. Wilkins
and the writer, just before midnight on April 3 1952, it was
totally invisible, though we made a special search for it with
the largest refractor in Europe (the Meudon 33-inch).

There is no doubt that the craterlet was invisible when we
made our observations, and four hours later T. A. Cragg, observing in America with a good 12½-inch reflector, was unable
to see even the most prominent details of the floor. What must
have happened is that mist spread from the east, covering
Steavenson's crater; by the time Cragg made his drawing, the
mist had extended all over the interior.

Although large telescopes are necessary for observations of this kind, the evidence is conclusive, and we are bound to accept a certain amount of activity on the floor of Plato. Nor is this the only case. Schickard, the great plain near the south-east limb shown in Plate VI, also provides us with fogs at times. In 1939, the writer was lucky enough to witness a particularly dense one; the whole crater was filled with whitish mist, which concealed all the normal floor-detail and even billowed over the lower sections of the wall. Another mist here was seen by Dr. Wilkins on August 31 1944, though all was normal by the following evening.

During the last twenty years, frequent mists have been seen inside the crater Timocharis by D. P. Barcroft, of Madera, and by several observers; and on March 27 1931 Robert Barker, observing from Cheshunt with his 12½-inch reflector, found the central mountain of the brilliant ray-crater Tycho 'a curious shade of grey', although the interior of the crater was in full shadow. It is worth remembering that W. R. Birt, President of the short-lived Selenographical Society, reported frequent mistiness inside Tycho between 1870 and 1880, while in recent times Barcroft has often found the floor 'strangely ill-defined'.

Another crater displaying some activity is Thales, near Endymion in the far north. In 1892, Professor Barnard, at the Lick Observatory, saw it filled with pale luminous haze, though all the surrounding features were perfectly sharp and normal; and the keenness of his eye cannot be questioned, as it was in this year that he discovered Amalthea, the tiny fifth satellite of Jupiter.

In 1902 a French astronomer, Charbonneaux, saw a small but unmistakable white cloud form close to Thætetus. Here again there seems no chance of error, as Charbonneaux was using the greatest refractor in Europe- the 33-inch at Meudon, the same instrument with which Dr. Wilkins and the writer made their Plato observations fifty years later.

All these observations point to low-lying mists in the lunar atmosphere, but perhaps the best example of a cloud was seen by F. H. Thornton on February 10 1949, near our old friend the Cobra-Head in the Herodotus Valley. Under good conditions, and using his 18-inch reflector, he saw a puff of whitish vapour obscuring details for some miles, while the surrounding surface remained perfectly clear and sharp. There is no doubt that this was due to local fog.

However, the most mist-affected area on the moon (apart from the interior of Plato) seems to be the southern part of the Mare Crisium, near the little crater Picard.

The Mare surface is fairly level, and on it there are only three craters of any size – Picard itself; Peirce, to the north; and Graham, a smaller formation to the north of Peirce. The region south and south-west of Picard was shown more or less featureless by all observers up to the beginning of the present century. Edmund Neison, author of the first accurate British lunar map, recorded only a few low ridges, and even Walter Goodacre, in his famous map, put in only three white spots. Just over twenty years ago Robert Barker, observing with his 12½-inch reflector at Cheshunt, in Hertfordshire, discovered a conspicuous 'quadrangle' made up of prominent craterlets connected by low ridges, where Mädler had shown nothing at all. Examination of old drawings showed that parts of the quadrangle had been seen from time to time, but never before had it appeared so conspicuous or so complete. Nowadays it can be seen with a very small telescope, and the whole region is dotted with craterlets and white spots which cannot possibly be missed. In 1949, the writer published a chart showing over seventy of them, and certainly they were not to be seen when Goodacre drew his map in 1910.

There are two possible explanations. Either the craterlets are of recent formation--which would prove that definite volcanic activity is still going on--or they were there all the time, hidden beneath a layer of mistiness. Such mist would not have to be thick. A very tenuous layer of haze would be enough to conceal the minute details underneath.

Of these two theories, the second appears much the more likely, and it is supported by dozens of independent observations of mists in the area. These observations go back eighty years to the time of Birt, who often noted that Graham, the crater south of Peirce, was totally invisible when it should have been obvious. This has also been found more recently--for instance, Dr. Wilkins could see no trace of it on May 12 1927, though it had been normal on May 11 and had reappeared faintly by May 13. Three times in 1948 the writer saw the whole area "misty grey and devoid of detail", with the surrounding surface sharp and clear-cut; R. M Baum, at Chester, saw a similar appearance twice, and on one night the 'quadrangle' alone was missing. its site being occupied by a nebulous white patch.

One object, a white spot closely west of Picard,[1] seems to be particularly strange. Most 'white spots' are really craterlets, too small to be seen clearly as such. This one, however, was thought by Birt not to be a craterlet at all, but some sort of surface deposit. Now and then it showed haziness and abnormal brilliance, and this has been confirmed in recent years, so that it appears to be able to send out a certain amount of vapour.

If lunar fogs are not made up of water-vapour, what are they? We can only guess, but carbon dioxide seems to be a reasonable answer. It is a heavy gas, so that even the feeble pull of the moon would be enough to hold it down, and we know that it is given off by volcanic eruptions, so that it may mark the last stages of activity of the dying volcanoes of the moon.

It is true, of course, that the mists are low-lying, tenuous and very local. Certainly we cannot compare them to the November fogs of England. Not only are they made up of different gases, but they are far thinner, and from the surface would appear to us as nothing more than very slight haze. Neither do they prove the existence of a moon-wide atmospheric mantle; and so let us see what other evidence can be collected.

Lunar meteors

Let us suppose that we are right in believing that an atmosphere exists, with a ground density of 1/10,000 of the earth's. This is about the maximum theoretical density – really, it is likely to be rather less–and it corresponds to what we normally call a laboratory vacuum Needless to say, no terrestrial organisms could possibly survive in it, even if it consisted of pure oxygen, which is certainly not the case. However, the moon's comparatively weak gravitational pull means that the air-density will only fall off very gradually as we rise above the surface.

[1] Numbered 7 in the writer's chart, B.A.A *Journal* (1949), **59**, 250.

Our own atmospheric pressure falls off by half every time we ascend three and a half miles, and, as every wartime flyer knows, it is impossible to go up much more than 2 miles without putting on an oxygen mask. But the moon's atmospheric pressure would only fall by half for every 21 miles' ascent, so that at an altitude of about 50 miles the corresponding densities of the two atmospheres would be equal. Higher than this, the lunar atmosphere would actually be the denser of the two!

Although such an air-mantle around the moon would be of no use for breathing, it would be most useful in another way—it would provide an effective screen against meteors, which would otherwise be a serious menace to any lunar colony.

We know that meteors travel round the sun in swarms. When the earth passes near or through a swarm, we see a shower of shooting-stars. Owing to the effect of simple perspective, all the meteors of any one shower seem to come from the same direction, and if we traced their path backwards across the sky they would all pass through a single point known as the shower 'radiant'. For instance, every year, about August 10, we see meteors radiating from the constellation Perseus. There are also 'sporadic meteors', not connected with any definite swarm, and as these may appear at any time and from any direction they cannot be predicted.

Ordinary-sized meteors generally appear at about 80 miles above the earth's surface, and disappear at about 50 miles. Larger ones may appear at altitudes greater than 100 miles, and strike the ground before they have been completely destroyed, although giants such as Peary's 36-ton mass or the object which hit Siberia in 1908 are very rare. Meteorites must be familiar to almost everyone; small specimens are common enough, and public collections are on view in various places. Several meteorites, for instance, may be seen in the Science Museum.

But assuming that the lunar atmosphere has a ground density of 1/10,000, the density at an altitude of 50 miles must be equal to that at the same height above the earth—and this is just where normal meteors disappear. Consequently, the atmosphere of the moon should be just as effective a shield as ours is, and we should be able to detect occasional luminous trails in it.

If the moon has no atmosphere at all, the rocky meteors should plummet straight down, unhindered in any way, and strike the surface, producing a bright flash or flare. Dr. LaPaz, of the University of New Mexico, has investigated the resulting flash-frequency, and has calculated that under these conditions a meteor weighing 10 lb. would produce a flash bright enough to be seen from the earth without using a telescope. There should, therefore, be about a hundred naked-eye flashes every year.

It need hardly be said that nothing of the kind is seen. Flares on the moon are very rare, and in any case not all of them can be attributed to meteors. Baum's red glow near Lichtenberg was certainly no meteor, and nor were the three 'active volcanoes' reported on the moon's dark side by Sir William Herschel in 1787, which were visible for two nights running. These last can only have been due to normal bright points, such as Aristarchus, illuminated by earthshine.

From time to time, however, observations which correspond to meteoric impacts are made; and one or two are worth quoting. On August 8 1948 A. J. Woodward, in America, saw "a small bright flash on the earthlit portion; it lasted for three seconds, turning from bluish white to greyish yellow – like a bright sparkle of frost on the ground". A bright speck inside Gassendi was seen by Dr. Wilkins on May 17 1951; it lasted for one second, and left a glow for perhaps two seconds more. On August 25 1950 Tsuneo Saheki, in Osaka, Japan, saw a stationary, yellowish-white flare, lasting for only about a quarter of a second. Perhaps the best example, however, was that seen by F. H. Thornton, using a 9-inch reflector, on April 15 1948, inside the much-studied Plato. Thornton's own description of it is as follows: "While I was examining Plato, I saw at its western rim, just inside the wall, a minute but brilliant flash of light. The nearest approach to a description of this is to say that it resembled the flash of an A.A. shell exploding in the air at a distance of about ten miles. In colour it was on the orange side of yellow. . . . My first thought was that it was due to a large fall of rock, but I changed my opinion when I realized that, close as it seemed to be to the mountain wall, it was possibly over half a mile away."[1]

It seems almost certain that this flash was really due to a meteoric fall. The only other plausible explanation - a volcanic eruption - is ruled out by the fact that it was of such short duration. After all, the meteor which fell in Siberia in 1908 blew down trees over 20 miles away, and had it not fallen in marshy, uninhabited tundra, the death-roll would have been colossal. The meteor which Thornton saw landing in Plato was probably no larger than this.

There is one marked difference, however, between the two falls. The Siberian meteor came down with a rush and a roar which was heard hundreds of miles away; the Plato meteor must have landed upon the moon in dead silence, despite the tremendous shock. The tenuous lunar air is certainly incapable of carrying sound-waves which would make any impression upon our ears.

Other flashes have been reported now and then, but most of them are rather doubtful; and it is perfectly clear that the observed number is not only less than might be expected from Dr. LaPaz' estimate, but startlingly less. Despite a systematic search carried out by Professor Haas and his colleagues in America, we have only four or five reliable flash-observations, and it looks very much as though the lunar atmosphere prevents ordinary-sized meteors from landing. This is borne out by the observations of luminous trails above the moon's surface, which may be due to 'shooting-stars' similar to those in our own air.

As the moon's atmosphere is probably denser than ours above an equivalent altitude of about 50 miles, meteors there would tend to appear higher up – perhaps 200 miles above the surface – so that the atmospheric shielding would be even more effective against bombardment, and falls such as that which produced Thornton's flash would be as rare as 'Siberian-type' falls with us.

In a letter to the writer dated September 11 1952, Dr. E. J. Öpik of Armagh Observatory, one of the world's foremost experts upon meteoric astronomy, wrote: "Lunar meteors are quite probable. Considering the surface gravity of the moon,

[1] B.A.A. *Journal* (1948), **57**, 142.

which leads to a six times' slower decrease of atmospheric density with height, the length of path and duration of meteor trails on the moon will be six times that on the earth, if a thin atmosphere exists. However, meteors the size of fireballs will penetrate the lunar atmosphere and hit the ground. The average duration of a meteor trail on the moon will be two to three seconds (as against half a second for the earth), and each trail should end with a flash when the meteor strikes the ground (because all meteors which can be observed in the lunar atmosphere, from such a distance, must be large fireballs). The average length of trail would be 75 miles, or one minute of arc –1/30 of the moon's diameter– and the meteors would therefore be very slow, short objects."

There are other difficulties in the way of our observing lunar meteors. Not only must they be of exceptional size, as Dr. Öpik points out, but they must also be against the non-lit or earthlit parts of the moon; we cannot hope to see them against the bright face, except in very rare cases.

Moreover, ordinary terrestrial meteors may prove troublesome. If it so happens that one of them plummets straight down towards the observer, in front of the moon, it will appear silhouetted against the lunar disk; but the disk is so small, compared with the vast expanse of sky, that the chances of a terrestrial meteor keeping right in front throughout its path are very small. It will almost always move clear of the moon for at least a portion of its path, and so betray its true nature, just as a bird flying towards us is unlikely to keep right in front of one small cloud.

What we must look for, therefore, is a faint point of light moving slowly over the moon's disk, more or less constant in brightness until it ends in a minute flash, and beginning rather abruptly. Professor Haas and his colleagues of the Association of Lunar and Planetary Observers have paid great attention to the problem, and have recorded a number of objects which answer to the required qualifications so well that they can be regarded as almost certain cases of lunar meteors. The average path-length of the objects observed proved to be 75 miles – in excellent agreement with the value given by Dr. Öpik; some left brief trails, and all were rather faint. Where colour could be seen at all, it generally seemed to be yellowish. Haas worked out the probable diameter of a lunar meteor seen by him in 1941, and arrived at a figure of 600 feet, similar to a terrestrial 'Siberian' fireball. To an observer on the moon itself, the brilliancy would have been comparable to that of the full moon seen from the earth.

It is true that we have so far no positive proof that the objects seen against the moon are not just ordinary terrestrial meteors;

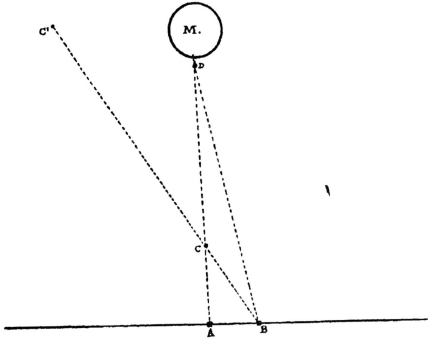

Fig. 9. Lunar and terrestrial meteors

but the odds against it are very great, and in any case we may hope for definite evidence before long. All that we need is simultaneous observation of a lunar meteor by two observers miles apart.

In Fig. 9, A and B represent two observers on the earth's surface; M is the moon, C a terrestrial meteor, and D a meteor in the lunar atmosphere. Observer A will see both C and D against the lunar disk; B will do so only for D, as C will appear at the point C″, well clear of the moon. If both A and B see the meteor D against the moon, it can only be a lunar meteor. The only way to obtain this proof is to keep on observing patiently, and wait for good fortune. This work is now going on in Britain, Europe, America and Japan, so that we may expect something definite within the next few years.

At all events, it seems likely that the atmosphere of the moon is dense enough to provide perfectly adequate protection against normal meteoric falls. It has often been said that manned lunar bases will have to be made thoroughly meteor-proof, but it now appears that the natural atmospheric blanket will save us the trouble.

Every now and then reports are received of dark objects passing in front of the moon. Bats and birds are usually responsible, although moths, aeroplanes, meteorological balloons and leaves are other culprits–at any rate, all such phenomena are definitely terrestrial in origin. Not long ago, an earnest observer sent in a report of "a curious dark object projected against the moon", which he evidently considered to be of great astronomical importance. Tactful questioning brought out the additional fact that it 'appeared to be flapping', after which there was really little more to be said.

Evidence from lunar shadows

Finally, some evidence of a general atmosphere may perhaps be gleaned from the lunar shadows, which are in general sharp and hard, but occasionally show strange anomalies.

As the sun rises over a lunar crater, it will first strike the outer west wall. With increasing altitude, the rays reach the inner east wall, and much of this inner wall is in full sunshine while the west wall still casts deep shadow over much of the crater-floor. The glare from the sunlit east wall is often strong enough to illuminate some of the interior features upon which the sun has not yet risen. W. R. Dawes, a well-known observer of the last century, was the first to point this out; in 1952, Dr. Steavenson repeated the observation, and distinctly saw the central mountains of the twin craters Godin and Agrippa by the reflected wall-light alone, and even detected the 'reversed' shadows cast by the peaks. He was, however, using a large telescope and a specially screened eyepiece, and even then the wall-lit mountains were not conspicuous.

A. C. Eliot Merlin, in Greece, had a different experience in 1909, when he was observing Mersenius, a large walled plain east of the Mare Humorum. He wrote: "The broad, irregular and sharply-indented shadows of the illuminated ridges, etc., in the neighbourhood, could be distinguished, apparently projected on the dark, unilluminated portion of the lunar surface. . . . The interior of Mersenius itself was perfectly dark, but the shadow of the east wall, only the top of which was illuminated by the rising sun, could be seen projected on the unlighted surface beyond the terminator The appearance was that of sharply-defined, inky-black shadows projected on a rusty black background. This effect must almost certainly have been caused by a dimly-lighted zone bordering the shadows. . . . The dimly-lit regions on which the shadows were cast were those which would themselves be shortly illuminated by the rising sun, thus forming a kind of dawn."[1] Here we have a sure case of lunar twilight.

Dr. Wilkins' observation of March 29 1939 was equally remarkable. On this occasion, the crater under study was Copernicus; and although the floor was in full shadow, the central mountain group appeared for about a quarter of an hour as a somewhat diffuse light spot, together with indications of the inner western terraces. The appearance then vanished, and the first solar rays did not strike the central peaks until three hours later. This must have been an atmospheric effect, perhaps very similar to Barker's earlier view of the greyish central peak in Tycho.

Although the lunar shadows are nearly always hard and jet-black, there are exceptions to the general rule, as is so often the case on the moon. For instance, Professor Haas considers that the sunrise shadow inside Eudoxus, north of the Caucasus Mountains, is always much darker than that inside its larger neighbour Aristoteles; and a curious, brownish-black border to the shadow inside Philolaus, a large crater not far from Pythagoras, has been seen by several observers, including the writer. It would be pointless to list all the recorded cases of shadow penumbræ, but it is clear that there are far too many of them to be explained away by faulty observation or tricks of the light.

---

[1] Eliot Merlin's telescope was an 8½-inch reflector The writer, who has used it, can vouch for its excellence.

Did the moon ever possess a dense atmosphere?

As we have seen, the moon could not hold down a dense atmosphere, because of its comparatively feeble gravitational pull. On the other hand, it is by no means certain that it ever had an extensive atmosphere at all. There is strong evidence that the earth's present atmosphere is not the original one it possessed when still molten. The hotter a molecule is, the faster it moves; and it seems probable that the earth lost nearly all its first atmosphere before it had cooled down. Later, when the crust solidified and vast quantities of water-vapour and other gases were given off, a new air-blanket was formed; and the oceans came into being later still, when the cooling had proceeded far enough to allow aqueous vapour to fall out of the moist atmosphere.

The history of the moon may have been roughly similar, but we cannot say for certain. We cannot even be sure that the moon and earth were originally one, and it is impossible to be definite about anything which happened in that long-ago period when the earth was still fiery and man belonged to the almost unbelievably remote future.

Whether or not the moon once had a thick atmosphere, most of it has now gone. However, a little remains–not enough to breathe, not even so much as is to be found in our own stratosphere, where terrestrial airmen cannot survive for a moment without oxygen-masks- but still, enough to be useful. It is almost certainly enough to protect lunar colonists from the dangers of meteoric bombardment, and it may also be enough to protect them from some of the undesirable solar rays which they will meet in outer space. Whether it is sufficient to help radio communication, or to be utilized for 'air-braking' a spaceship, is much more doubtful, and we may not know for sure until the first interplanetary journey has been made. At all events, we know that the moon does not totally lack atmosphere. The oft-repeated statement that "the moon is a dead, airless world" is nearly as wide of the mark as Kepler's idea of a planet peopled by men.

CHAPTER 10

THE MOULDING OF THE SURFACE

SINCE the moon is comparatively close to us, our ignorance of its past history is really rather surprising. Geologists have traced back the story of the earth as far as Cambrian times, 500 million years ago; and if asked to draw up a map of our world as it must have been some 100 million years ago, they could certainly produce something at least reasonably accurate.

We know comparatively little about the story of the moon. This is largely because we cannot yet examine the surface close at hand; when we are able to obtain specimens of the surface materials, a great many puzzles may well be solved. Another point is that we have to delve back much further into the past. By the time that terrestrial life began, and the first fossils were laid in the Cambrian rocks, the active existence of the moon was almost at an end; the surface had become set and almost, though not quite, changeless. It is sometimes difficult to remember that the youngest lunar craters are probably older than the oldest terrestrial fossils.

A glance at the moon's face shows us many familiar features. Mountains, valleys and faults abound there, and there is no reason to suppose that they are fundamentally different from the corresponding formations on the earth. They, at least, present no problems. The craters and seas are the main puzzles. Once we know definitely how they came into being, we have the key to all lunar history.

The 'volcanic fountain'

As the surface is so obviously volcanic, it is tempting to regard the craters as nothing more than old volcanoes, even though they do not resemble terrestrial volcanic craters either in form or in size. Two English astronomers, Nasmyth and Carpenter, produced a very attractive theory in 1874, which is well worth describing. They pictured a central volcano, erupting violently and showering débris in a ring all round it–a sort of volcanic fountain. The matter ejected from the central orifice built up the circular wall, and as the eruptions became less violent, inner terraces were formed. In the dying stages of activity, when the explosions were only just powerful enough to lift material out of the vent, the central peak was built up. Craters without central peaks could be explained by supposing that the explosions ceased rather suddenly, so that the floor was covered by lava which welled up from inside the moon.

This theory seems very plausible at first sight. The terraces, the hill-top craters, the flooded craters and even the famous plateau, Wargentin, are accounted for; and the ringed formations do give the superficial impression of having been built up in this way Unfortunately, there are a great many fatal objections. It is beyond all belief that a circular wall over 100 miles in diameter, and sharply defined (as is the case with Clavius, for instance), could have been formed in such a fashion, and in any case the inner slopes are far too gentle. Moreover, the central peaks are always considerably lower than the rampart, which would not be expected on Nasmyth's theory, and many craters whose floors show no trace of flooding by later lava have no central peaks at all (as with Harpalus, the crater which achieved fame when it was selected as the landing-ground for the first space-ship in the film *Destination Moon*).

The explanation given for the bright rays is equally untenable. Nasmyth and Carpenter considered that the crust of the moon had cracked in places, much as a glass globe does when it is struck, and that lava had oozed out of the cracks, forming the rays; but it is now certain that the rays are mere surface deposits, not connected with fissures of any kind. In fact, there are so many weak points about the theory that we are reluctantly forced to abandon it altogether, attractive though it seems.

The ice theory

Before going on to modifications of the volcanic theory, it will be interesting to examine some of the other ideas which have been put forward, and which do not bring in volcanic activity at all. The two most important are Ericson's ice theory and Gruithuisen's meteoric hypothesis.

H

The first of these was originally suggested by Ericson, of Norway, in 1885. It was supported by S. E. Peal, a tea-planter of Ceylon, who wrote a booklet about it four years later, and more recently by Fauth, of Berlin, who died as lately as 1943. It supposes the craters to be nothing more than frozen lakes of water, and, in Peal's own words: "As the lakes slowly solidified in the cooling crust, the water vapour rising from them formed a local, dome-shaped atmosphere, which became a vast condensed snowy margin and piled as a vast ring." This means that the Maria are actual sea-surfaces, solidified, and that the entire moon is coated with a thick layer of ice. Fauth, the only modern supporter of this strange idea, considered that the ice came from outer space in a 'cosmic rain', forming a layer round the moon's rocky core over 100 miles thick

Of course, the whole theory is completely unsound. The temperature of the daytime hemisphere of the moon can rise above that of boiling water, which is not very suitable for the permanent existence of either ice or snow; and in any case an icy crater-rampart would not keep its shape for long Ice acts as a plastic, not as a rigid solid, and a wall made up of it would soon flatten out under its own weight. This effect can be noted after any heavy winter snowfall in England.

The glaciation theory may seem strange, but an even more peculiar idea was seriously put forward only ten years or so ago by a certain Herr Weissberger, of Vienna, who solved the whole problem very easily, simply by denying that there were any lunar mountains or craters at all. He attributed them merely to storms and cyclones in a dense lunar atmosphere, and appeared most surprised when the astronomical world failed to treat him with due respect![1]

[1] It must not be supposed that Herr Weissberger has the monopoly of weird ideas. As recently as 1937 there was a flourishing Flat Earth Society in London, and some of their arguments are worth recording, as follows: (1) There is no South Pole (2) Besides being flat, the earth stands still (3) Mars is only 15,000 miles away, and is much too small to be inhabited. (4) It is quite impossible to measure the distance of the moon. In 1949, the British Interplanetary Society was deluged with leaflets written by a Margaret Missen, of Edinburgh, who regarded the earth as both flat and stationary "because we should otherwise be made giddy by the movement of the ground, and digestive processes would be impossible" It was also added that ships and trains would be unable to make any headway if they were trying to move in a direction opposite to that of a rotating earth The opinions of this latter writer about the moon remain – fortunately – unpublished.

The meteoric theory

Unlike Ericson's walls of ice, the impact theory, which attributes the craters to the results of meteoric bombardment of the lunar surface, has received a surprising amount of support. It was first put forward by Gruithuisen, a German astronomer, in 1824, it was then forgotten, revived by a popular English astronomical writer, R. A. Proctor (though he himself abandoned it in later life), and is now often met with in textbooks. In the Dome of Discovery at the 1951 Festival of Britain it was even presented as an established fact. However, there are very few modern practical observer who have any use for it, and careful examination shows that it is just as untenable as Nasmyth and Carpenter's volcanic fountain.

It is perfectly true that a large meteorite will cause a crater-like scar when it lands on a plastic surface, and this scar will be more or less circular even if the missile lands at an angle, as we can demonstrate by the simple experiment of firing air-gun pellets into sand. There are several such formations on the earth. The 'Coon Butte' crater, in Arizona, is almost circular, and not much less than a mile in diameter, with a wall which rises 150 feet above the surrounding plain, and this is certainly due to a meteoric fall, as thousands of small meteoric fragments have been picked up nearby; and it is certainly very old, though the date of its formation is not known even approximately.

Other meteor craters are found in the United States, Arabia, Australia and the Estonian island of Oésel, in the Baltic, but the largest specimen so far discovered is the Chubb crater in Northern Quebec, near Lake Ungava. It was first found in 1950 by the Canadian prospector after whom it is named, and described by him as being "an immense hole looking like a great tea-cup tilted at a steep angle".

As soon as the discovery was reported, a Toronto expedition, headed by Dr. Victor Meen, went to investigate. It was found that the great crater is 2 miles across and 1,500 feet deep, part of the floor being occupied by a lake. Once again, we cannot tell how old the Chubb crater is; but it must have been formed well before the dawn of recorded history.

The only really large meteorite to fall in recent years landed

in Siberia, in 1908, with a roar audible 1,000 miles away. Had
it fallen five hours or so earlier, it would have scored a direct
hit upon the city of St. Petersburg (now Leningrad), and the
death-roll would have been colossal. Unfortunately the first
scientific expeditions did not arrive at the site until years later,
due principally to the unsettled state of affairs in Russia about
that time, and as the meteorite fell in marshy ground the crater
it made has now largely filled up.

We regard the Coon Butte, Chubb and Siberian craters as
big, but they would cut a very poor figure on the moon; all
three could be accommodated inside Piazzi Smyth, the minor
walled plain between Pico and Piton on the Mare Imbrium. In
any case, they are no more like lunar formations than the
terrestrial volcanoes are.

Objections to the meteoric theory

The central mountains are particularly hard to explain by
the impact theory. R. B. Baldwin, of the United States, who
published a valuable book in 1949 in which the idea was de-
fended, attributed them to the rebounding of the surface layers
immediately after the meteorite struck them. It is extremely
difficult to picture the mighty complex mountains of the great
walled plains being formed in this way, and all large formations,
such as Clavius, would be expected to show at least traces of
a central mound—which is not so. It is often stated that bomb-
craters of the last war showed similar peaks, but the writer, who
saw a great many crater-pits, never found anything even re-
motely resembling a lunar-type peak.

Neither did Baldwin take the lunar atmosphere into account.
We know that even the present tenuous air-blanket forms an
effective shield, and in the far-off days when the craters were
being born it is only reasonable to suppose that the atmosphere
was at least as dense as it is now, even though we have no
actual proof. Unless we suppose that the moon was obligingly
left airless just when the meteors were preparing to bombard
it, the whole theory must be rejected.

Another objection to the meteor theory, this time a fatal one,
is that the craters are not distributed at random all over the
surface. When one crater breaks into another, it is always the

larger crater which is damaged; and although it is true that the larger meteors would in general have fallen first, there would be at least a few exceptions to the general rule, whereas actually there are none. Twins, such as Helicon and Le Verrier on the Mare Imbrium, are common, and so are double craters such as Sirsalis-Bertaud, south of Grimaldi. Moreover, the largest formations tend to line themselves up Look, for instance, at Langrenus, Vendelinus, Petavius and Furnerius, along the western limb.

The volcanic theories explain these chains reasonably enough by supposing that the craters broke out along well-defined lines of weakness in the crust; the meteor theory has to imagine four exceptional-sized meteors falling, at different times, in a perfect line.[1] Ptolemæus is the northernmost member of a similar chain, and there are many others equally well marked. Baldwin accounted for these in a curious way. He stated that the lines of walled plains were not really well marked at all, and only appeared so because the sun, shining from either east or west, produced shadow effects which gave a false impression! It can only be said that no practical observer is likely to agree with this view.

Even more striking are the smaller crater-chains, which occur in great numbers. The so-called 'cleft' of Hyginus, as we have seen, is one, and there are dozens of others within the reach of a very small telescope. They vary in form. Sometimes the craters are separate and complete; in other cases the common walls have been broken down so that the floors are connected, and the whole feature takes on the appearance of a valley with raised banks and tell-tale bulges along its length.

Volcanically, such formations are only to be expected; but how can we explain them by falling meteors? Either we must suppose that the meteors have a surprising ability to line themselves up with geometrical accuracy, or we must picture them landing in orderly 'family parties'. The odds against either of these ideas are impossibly great.

Baldwin overcame this difficulty in a way which was most

---

[1] These four formations are not equal in age Petavius, for instance, is obviously younger than Vendelinus. The chain is continued northwards, and ends at Endymion.

ingenious, though not at all convincing He admitted that the
chain-craters were volcanic, and went on to claim that they
were different in form from all other lunar craters. Unfortunately, however, the individual craters of a chain are fundamentally just like ordinary craters, and so the argument does
not carry much weight.

There are also the 'hill-top' craters, perched on the tops of
the central peaks of many walled plains If the peaks themselves
were volcanic in nature, nothing would be more likely after all,
terrestrial volcanoes invariably show them. On the impact
theory, however, they could not be explained except by sheer
chance hits.

Baldwin listed twelve 'hill-top' craters, and calculated that if
they were due to meteorites happening to fall right on the tops
of the peaks, there should be about fifteen known. Using two
of the largest refracting telescopes in Europe,[1] Dr. Wilkins and
the writer discovered several new ones in the course of a few
nights' work; over forty are now known, and there can be no
doubt that they are really quite common, although they are so
small that they are hard to see except with very high powers.
We can therefore reject the 'hit or miss' idea, particularly as
the hill-top craters are invariably central on their peaks, not
placed to one side; and it is clear that, all things considered, all
forms of the impact theory have so many weak points that there
is no choice but to abandon them completely [2]

[1] The 33-inch at the Observatory of Meudon, and the 25-inch Newall telescope
at Cambridge University Observatory
[2] G Fielder recently communicated to the writer an ingenious modification of
the impact theory, which avoids some, though not all, of the traps of the more
generally accepted version. In a letter dated October 10 1952 he wrote "My
theory assumes the most recent ideas on planetary formation, as put forward by
the German physicist C. von Weizsacker Von Weizsacker's theory, which
accounts for many more of the peculiarities of the solar system than any preceding theory, says that the moon was captured by the earth after having been
formed by the coagulation of small, solid particles, rotating as a 'dust cloud'.
Before it was captured, therefore, it must have been wandering through the plane
of our planetary system A large body (of which there are plenty in the asteroid
belt) was attracted towards the moon and forced to disintegrate into several
parts, because of the moon's pull Having an increasing velocity, by virtue of the
moon's gravitational attraction, these huge parts, up to 100 miles in diameter,
rushed towards the surface of the moon, and, with inconceivable devastation,
wrought the many features that are now to be seen. First, the seas, then the
larger craters were formed by matter thrown off as splashes from these great
crash sites The fresh impacts, in turn, caused innumerable craterlets to be
stamped over the lunar terrain. At the same time were formed the ray-systems

Tidal theories

Ice-banks and meteors being equally out of the question, what other agencies can we introduce without resorting to vulcanism in some form?

Some theories make use of the tides. One of these has recently been put forward by Boneff, of Bulgaria, though it is not really much more than a modification of an earlier idea due to Professor W. H. Pickering According to Boneff, the craters were formed when the moon's crust had just solidified, and the moon, much closer to the earth than it is now, was still rotating on its axis comparatively quickly. The hot, viscid interior was much more affected by the earth's tidal pull than was the thin crust, and so at each revolution of the moon on its axis the molten lava surged upwards, breaking through the weak points of the crust. The action was rather like that of a pump. Gradually the large craters were built up; as the moon receded and its axial spin slowed down, the tidal effects lessened, so that the formations produced were smaller At last the crust became too solid to be broken by the surging lava inside, so that crater-building ceased altogether.

Boneff stated that the earth's crust was not then solid enough to register any similar craters, but did not rule out the possibility of the moon still affecting the frequency of terrestrial earthquakes. Moreover, if it is agreed that the moon will one day approach the earth once more (as seems more or less certain), he considered that it may yet be capable of covering our lands and drying seas with lunar-type craters, before it is at last torn apart by our gravitational pull. The last paragraph of his paper is worth quoting: "An earth without a moon, surrounded by a ring of minute bodies and entirely covered with formations of the lunar type, except perhaps at the poles – that is the probable state of the earth-moon system, if it still exists, after many thousands of millions of years."

It is a sombre picture, but not one which we need take too seriously. Apart from the fact that the earth's crust is now much

and the gigantic cracks, generally initiated by a string of comparatively small meteors falling together. In short, nearly all the observable lunar features were moulded over some definite region of time in the past."

too thick to be disturbed by even a nearby moon, the whole theory is basically unsound. The central mountains cannot possibly be accounted for; nor can the hill-top and wall-craters; the lunar landscape is much harder and sharper than would be the case if it had been moulded by the gentle surging of lava; and there are other objections too numerous to mention.

Other theories

Ingolf Ruud, of Norway, has recently put forward a 'direct contraction' theory. According to him, it was the crust of the moon which contracted round a less-yielding interior, so that it thinned and stretched at its weaker points, with the formation of circular craters. On Ruud's theory the smallest formations are the oldest, and the greatest of all the circular plains, the Mare Imbrium, is the youngest. This flies in the face of observation, and as neither the central peaks nor any other features of the craters can be satisfactorily accounted for, the theory must be at once rejected.

A. Fillias, of France, has suggested a similar mechanism of formation, due not to the contraction of the crust, but to the expansion of the interior However, there is no reason to suppose that the moon's core has any tendency to expand–quite the reverse and, in any case, Fillias' theory has all the weak points of Ruud's.

In 1917, D P. Beard propounded a strange theory in which he claimed that the whole surface of the moon had once been covered with an immense ocean, and that the craters were merely limestone formations similar to our own coral atolls. This, regretfully, must be placed in the same class as Herr Weissberger's atmospheric cyclones!

The only other recent serious theory which avoids both the Scylla of meteors and the Charybdis of vulcanism is that of K. H. Engel, of the United States, who considered that the craters were formed by the spontaneous solidification and crystallization of a fairly shallow lava-layer. However, it does not seem very likely that the giant walled plains could have been formed in any such way.

All things considered, the non-volcanic theories have failed us. Each has fatal weaknesses, and we are forced back, if not to

Nasmyth and Carpenter's delightful 'fiery fountain', at least to igneous action of some sort.

Volcanic theories

The 'bubble' idea, put forward by Robert Hooke as long ago as 1665, is worthy of mention. Hooke supposed that the craters were formed by gas bubbles beneath the crust, which forced the surface upwards and caused it to fracture, leaving great scars; we can see effects rather like this in boiling tar. Here again the central mountains present an obvious difficulty, but in recent years H G. Tomkins, J. E. Spurr and others have proposed theories which bear some resemblance to Hooke's, and enable us to build up a general picture which may contain at least part of the truth.

How the craters may have been formed

Let us go back to the time when the moon had a comparatively thin but more or less solid crust, overlying a layer of molten, viscous lava. Tidal effects, due to the pull of the earth, would result in crustal strains, and set up general activity. At any weak point, lava would force its way through the crust to form a 'feed-pipe', and before long the whole surrounding area would be lifted by an uprush of gas, forming a dome.

If the pressure was not strong enough for any further development, the eruption would cease and the dome would remain; but generally so much gas would be forced out through the feed-pipe that the pressure below would relax abruptly, and the dome would subside with comparative suddenness. This would lower it into the hot lava, and the 'skin' of the old dome would melt.

This process might be repeated several times, with the eventual formation of walls low above the outside surface, but high above the continually remelted interior. Terraces would also be formed; and as the floor gradually congealed, hills and minor craters would arise in it. Often the dying stages of ejection from the feed-pipe would result in the building-up of a massive central elevation, naturally lower than the original surface level; in other cases, a final phase of melting inside the now deep hollow would destroy all interior detail, even to the central peak (if one had ever been formed). In one instance, Wargentin, the rising rush of lava was trapped when its lower escape-vent became blocked, so that it had to solidify where it was.

The early surface activity was naturally the most violent, because the moon was then at its hottest and tidal strains were at their maximum; so that the oldest craters were the largest, and were broken into by the smaller ones which arose later. Craters tended to appear along lines of crustal weakness, so that they formed strings and chains, and very often two similar weak points in the crust resulted in twin craters.

At a fairly early stage in the history of the surface moulding, though probably after the formation of the oldest walled plains which still remain visible (such as Janssen), one or two particularly violent uplifts and subsidences took place, forming circular plains of great size. Probably there were one or two which were either blotted out later, or are still to be seen as the lighter, patchier and less regular seas such as the Mare Fœcunditatis and the Oceanus Procellarum.

The tremendous cataclysm which resulted in the Mare Imbrium gave rise to a complete remelting of the crust over a large area, and lavæ rolled across the plain in the direction of the Oceanus Procellarum–making it impossible for us to be sure now whether the Oceanus was due to an earlier subsidence, or is merely a lava overflow from the Mare Imbrium. The Mare Humorum, definitely a separate subsidence product, had its northern wall battered by the rolling lava either then or earlier, so that the wall was finally breached to such an extent that the two lava-streams met and mingled. The mountain wall between the Mare Imbrium and the slightly older Mare Serenitatis also came in for rough treatment, but was so massive that it managed to survive, except for one stretch between the modern Apennines and Caucasus; probably it acted as a huge groyne, protecting the westward area from more extensive remelting.

Other dome-collapses gave rise to the Mare Nectaris, the Mare Crisium and the Mare Humboldtianum, although the smaller lunabase areas, such as the Lacus Somniorum and the Mare Vaporum, were no more than lava overflows. Craters such as Letronne and Fracastorius, bordering the remelted areas, were badly damaged on their 'seaward' sides, and craters which had once existed on the collapsed regions were either badly reduced--as Stadius has been--or totally overwhelmed.

As the tremendous upheavals died down, smaller craters began to appear on the solidifying floors of the greatest domes. Some, such as Archimedes on the Mare Imbrium, were born before the surface had cooled sufficiently to allow them to become very deep, so that their floors were rapidly remelted and became smooth and featureless; others, such as Copernicus and Eratosthenes, were not born until much later, by which time the old collapse-areas had become about as solid as the original surface had been before the great seas came into being.

Gradually the uplifts and collapses became smaller and less frequent, as the inner lava cooled and the increasing distance between moon and earth lessened the tidal effects; and at last crater formation virtually ceased.

It is important to remember that during its active period the moon must have had an atmosphere, although this atmosphere was not at all like the air of the earth--volcanoes give off tremendous amounts of gas -and so much material was drawn out from under the crust that cavities were left. Consequently, the crust crumpled, resulting in the formation of all the various features with which we on earth are familiar because of the shrinkage of our own planet. Finally, when activity had nearly ceased, came explosions from a few of the still living craters, which deposited long streams of ashy powder upon the now solid and almost cold surface.

The writer is well aware that this picture of the surface moulding leaves much to be desired. However, it does at least account for the craters, their distribution, their chains and their floor-details, which neither the impact nor the various tidal theories can do. Moreover, it puts the 'seas' in their proper place, as nothing more than exceptionally large craters or mere lava-overflows. Shaler, the American geologist, once suggested that the seas were meteoric in origin and the ordinary craters volcanic, but there seems no reason at all for such a distinction.

The problem of the bright rays

The rays present one of the main problems, and although
there can be little doubt that they are due to volcanic ash, it is
not at all clear why they stretch for such vast distances in such
regular lines.

Nasmyth and Carpenter thought that the rays were caused
by lava welling out from surface cracks; Tomkins, who put
forward a theory of the surface in which he made use of the
quiet fissuring of 'laccoliths', or domes of volcanic rock, thought
that they were due to salt. Fauth, true to his ice-banks, seriously
suggested that they were lines of ice-crystals blown out from
cracks in the walls of the craters responsible! On the meteor
theory, the rays were formed at the same time as the central
crater of their system; but as they pass over all other surface
features without deviating in the slightest from their paths, this
would make the ray-craters the very youngest on the entire
moon, which is obviously not the case. Ash-spraying, marking
the final gestures of dying volcanoes, is the only reasonable
answer, but the various mysteries of the bright rays are not
likely to be solved until we can actually inspect them close at
hand.

One final point should be made. Although all the great craters
of the moon must be volcanic structures, it is quite possible that
some of the smaller ones, particularly the rimless objects seen
by Dr. Wilkins and the writer in large numbers through the
great telescopes of Meudon and Cambridge, really are due to
meteoric impacts – or even to the falls of rocks hurled high in
the air by volcanoes. (It must be remembered that an explosion
on the moon would lift material much higher than on the earth,
as the gravitational pull is so much less.) Meteor craters certainly occur on the earth, and as the two atmospheres are about
equally effective as screens we may well expect to find some of
them scattered over the moon as well.

As we look now at the moon's quiet, tranquil surface, it is
hard to picture the scene in those distant days when the craters
were being formed. The whole moon must have been a smoking,
seething mass, a veritable inferno; and as there was atmosphere,
there must have been deafening noise, too. Volcanoes roared

defiance at the heavens, and raging gas-flames cast lurid, flickering lights here and there as the surface twisted and heaved. As the years passed in their millions, the fury died down, until at last the roar of a volcano was only occasional; and at about the time that the first sea-creatures appeared in the warm oceans of our own world, the moon subsided into its long sleep – a sleep from which it will only be awakened by the coming of man.

CHAPTER 11

CHANGES ON THE SURFACE

THE appearance of the moon changes from night to night, almost from hour to hour. As the shadows shift, new features are brought into view and old ones vanish, so that a crater which juts out strikingly from the terminator one evening may be difficult to make out at all twenty-four hours later. To know any one formation really well, an observer must study it under all possible angles of illumination.

Obviously, these rapid changes are not real. They are due to the movement of the sun across the lunar sky; and by working out the position of the terminator in advance, we can more or less forecast what will be seen when we go to the telescope. Permanent changes on the surface are very rare, and after a century and a half of careful observation we can only point to one certain case and a few possibilities.

Mists are not unusual. It is probable, for instance, that the comparatively recently discovered craterlets in the Mare Crisium, near Picard, are not new; they were there before, but hidden from view by fog. The variations inside Plato are also due to local mists. One or two of the large dark-floored craters, such as Grimaldi and Endymion, show regular changes each lunation; certain parts of their floors darken under a rising sun, while others become lighter in hue. But cases where new craters have been formed, or old ones have vanished or changed their shape, are almost unknown.

However, it must be remembered that exact observations have only been made over the past 150 years, and before 1866 there were only four observers–Schröter, Löhrmann, Mädler (with Beer) and Schmidt–who can be considered reliable. A century and a half is not a long period on the astronomical time-scale, so it is hardly surprising that few permanent changes have been recorded as yet.

The mystery of Linné

The classical case is that of Linné, on the Mare Serenitatis, probably the most famous and certainly the most-studied object on the entire moon. Lunar observers in general have every reason to be grateful to it, since it was the direct cause of the reawakening of interest in the moon from 1866 onwards.

Linné is easy to observe. It lies fairly near the apparent centre of the disk, so that there are no obvious foreshortening effects; and moreover it lies in level country, with nothing near it except for a few low ridges and mounds. Löhrmann, in 1834, described it as "the second most conspicuous crater on the plain . . . it has a diameter of about six miles,[1] is very deep, and can be seen under all conditions of illumination". Mädler, about the same time, wrote: "The deepness of the crater must be considerable, for I have found an interior shadow when the sun had attained 30°. I have never seen a central mountain on the floor." Both observers drew it, measured it, and used it as a reference point; and it appears as a conspicuous crater on six drawings made by Schmidt between 1841 and 1843.

All this was definite enough. Yet on October 16 1866, Schmidt was examining the Mare Serenitatis when he suddenly realized that Linné had disappeared. Where the old deep crater had stood, all that remained was a small whitish patch. It was a startling discovery, equivalent to the complete disappearance of a town such as Nottingham from the map of England.

Schmidt's announcement caused a world-wide sensation. Up to then, Mädler's view that the moon was dead and changeless had been accepted without question, and astronomers were not at once inclined to change their opinions. Hundreds of telescopes were pointed at Linné, and during the next few years a great many drawings were made of it. The results were not in complete agreement, but at least it was clear that the deep crater described by the old observers had utterly gone. In its place was a whitish patch, perhaps slightly variable in extent, and containing a minute object which was sometimes described as a craterlet and sometimes as a hill.

[1] Lohrmann actually said "somewhat more than one mile", but the old German mile is equal to 4¼ of ours. The most conspicuous crater on the whole Mare Serenitatis is, of course, Bessel, 12 miles in diameter and over 3,000 feet deep.

Later observations have not thrown any additional light on the problem. A shallow depression some 6 miles across, described by several early observers soon after Schmidt's announcement, seems to have disappeared now; the white patch surrounding the modern craterlet is probably a surface deposit of some sort, as it increases slightly in size during a lunar eclipse, when a wave of cold sweeps over the moon, and from time to time mistiness has been seen nearby. F. H. Thornton has recently examined Linné with his powerful telescope, and has found that it is now a dome, with a minute, deep central craterlet; this was confirmed by the writer in 1953.

Some people have flatly denied that any change has taken place. Quite frankly, this is simply flying in the face of all the evidence. It is not as though Linné lay in a crowded part of the moon. It stands by itself, in a particularly level area; and to suppose that both Löhrmann and Mädler drew, measured and described a deep crater which did not really exist is beyond all possibility. Moreover, Schmidt, the best lunar observer of his time, observed Linné both before and after its metamorphosis, and had not the slightest hesitation in stating that a radical change had taken place.

The earlier charts are not helpful. Cassini's map of 1692 shows something in the right position, but the map is very rough; and only one of Schröter's sketches has come down to us–undoubtedly there were others, but all Schröter's notebooks were burned with his observatory at Lilienthal. The one surviving drawing was made only to show the bright rays which cross the Mare Serenitatis. The other details are only roughed in; and although both Linné and Bessel are shown as spots, the sketch cannot be said to prove anything at all.

However, the evidence as it stands is absolutely conclusive. Some time between 1843 and 1866, a 6-mile crater, 1,000 feet or more deep, vanished from the moon, to be replaced by an insignificant craterlet surrounded by a white nimbus. The main problem is to find out just why it happened.

As the surface of the moon is subjected to great extremes of temperature, the rocks must expand and contract to some extent. This probably results in a certain amount of 'exfoliation', or flaking away of their surfaces, as occurs upon the earth. On the other hand, the effect must be very minor, due to the total absence of moisture, and cannot possibly account for the disappearance of a large crater in less than twenty-five years.

A meteoric fall has also been suggested. This is a possibility, but it would be a very strange coincidence if a plunging meteor scored a direct hit upon the only crater for miles around; and it seems much more likely that there was a 'moonquake', or ground tremor, due to internal forces, violent enough to cause the crater-walls to cave in, with powdering of the nearby surface. Whether the present tiny craterlet is an entirely new formation, it is impossible to say. One of the first acts of the early space-travellers will certainly be to go and examine Linné; but until this is done, it is unlikely that the mystery will be fully cleared up.

Other lost craters

There is one other similar case. On the western border of the Mare Crisium, Schröter described "a large distinct crater, with bright walls and a dusky floor, visible under all lighting conditions". He named it Alhazen, measured its diameter as 23 miles, and used it as a reference-point, so that it must have been a conspicuous object. By Madler's time it had completely disappeared, and all that remained was an ill-defined depression between two mountain peaks. As he was unable to find Schröter's crater, Madler transferred the name to a different crater some way to the south, so that the modern Alhazen is not the same object as that described by Schröter.

It is true that the southern Mare Crisium is subject to occasional fogs, but these fogs never extend into the highlands, and we can rule out the possibility that the original crater is still in existence. The whole area always appears perfectly sharp and clear-cut. The evidence in favour of change is not conclusive, as in the case of Linné, but in spite of his clumsy draughtsmanship Schröter made very few bad mistakes; he was a painstaking observer, and never drew anything that he was not certain of having seen. It is hard to picture him drawing and measuring a prominent object which did not really exist, and in any case Tobias Mayer's map, drawn over twenty years before, shows a well-marked crater in the corresponding position.

I

If the walls and floors of Schröter's Alhazen had changed colour until they merged with the outside country, the crater would still be betrayed by its wall-shadow under a low sun; and once again, the most likely explanation is that a sublunar disturbance caused its walls to cave in.

Close to the conspicuous crater Alpetragius, just outside the wall of Alphons and not far from the middle of the disk, Beer and Mädler drew two craterlets. One of them, lettered 'd', was said to be about 5 miles across, and the other rather smaller. The smaller crater is still there, but the larger is not. Once again, Schmidt was responsible for detecting the discrepancy. In 1868 he reported that the former crater had become a bright white spot, not unlike the new Linné, and this is how it appears to-day. Here again the evidence in favour of alteration is quite strong, but not conclusive. The formation is, and always was, small, and only Beer and Mädler drew it as a distinct crater. Schröter cannot help us, as all his drawings of this region were destroyed.

Whatever the truth about Schroter's Alhazen and the craterlet near Alpetragius, we have one certain case – Linné – of a formation which has more or less disappeared. There is no known case of a new crater having come into being. Several have been reported, but all seem highly dubious.

Reported 'new' formations

Cassini, the ringed plain near the Alps which contains the Washbowl, was strangely left out of the early maps, and was first drawn in 1692 by J. D. Cassini, after whom it is named. It has been suggested that it is a new formation, but this is definitely not the case. Quite apart from the fact that it looks ancient, it is not at all conspicuous, and we can well understand its being overlooked by the early observers with their low-powered telescopes.

The only moderately convincing case does not concern a true crater at all, but a rimless depression close to the famous crater-cleft of Hyginus, and known as Hyginus N. It was first seen on May 27 1877 by Klein, who described it as a rimless depression 3 miles across, filled with shadow under oblique lighting. This corresponds to the modern appearance. Klein had often observed the region during the previous twelve years without seeing a trace of it; and as it was also absent from all the maps, Klein concluded that it was definitely new. Schmidt had drawn the region over thirty times during the preceding thirty years, and in the position of Klein's N he had sometimes recorded a small dark spot, sometimes a bright spot and sometimes nothing at all, so that he too was certain that a change had occurred.

A smaller depression not far from N was also thought to be of recent origin. Admittedly, both formations are small, but it is not easy to see how both Mädler and Löhrmann could have overlooked them, as they had drawn the area on many occasions. Moreover, there still seem to be traces of local activity in the region. Mists have been seen from time to time, and on April 4 1944 Dr. Wilkins saw that N was much darker than usual, while the southern edge of the great Hyginus crater-valley was bordered by a narrow dark band for more than 8 miles along its length.

The large walled plain Cleomedes, just north of the Mare Crisium, contains a small crater considered by Schroter to have been formed about October 1789 – since he had missed it previously, and saw it quite clearly afterwards. Judging from the general appearance of the formation, such a thing seems most unlikely, and as the crater concerned is not at all prominent we must conclude that Schröter merely overlooked it. Perhaps he was not at fault, as mists have been periodically reported in the area, and when Schröter made his first drawings the crater may have been hidden.

A similar case is that of Halley, a small crater on the borders of the great walled plain Hipparchus (its twin, closely north-west of it, is named Hind). No floor-detail is shown by Löhrmann or Mädler. A famous photograph taken by Lewis Rutherfurd in 1865 shows one distinct craterlet. At the moment, there are two; and it has been thought that the second, not shown on the Rutherfurd photograph, has been formed since 1865. It is much more likely, however, that it was obscured at the moment when the photograph was taken.

Changes in brightness

Variations in colour and brilliancy are also known. For instance, a blackish area on the floor of the great crater Petavius,

seen by all the early observers, cannot now be traced. An even
better instance is that of Werner, the northern 'twin' of a pair
of craters outside the western wall of Regiomontanus (the other
'twin' is Aliacensis) Beer and Mädler stated that one particular
spot on the floor was as brilliant as any part of the lunar surface,
and they deliberately rated it equal to Aristarchus, the glittering
crater which has so often been mistaken for an active volcano.
Although the spot is still fairly bright, it is nothing like so
brilliant as Aristarchus, and has definitely faded during the last
100 years.

The Messier twins

Finally, let us consider the craters which are supposed to have
changed form since lunar observing began. Only two cases are
worth mentioning; and the more important is that of Messier,
which lies on the Mare Fœcunditatis, not far from the lunar
equator.

Messier is the western member of a pair of small craterlets,
noteworthy because two curious streamers of ash extend from
them towards the Mare coast. The eastern 'twin' used to be
called Messier A, but has now been renamed Pickering. The
two can always be recognized without difficulty owing to the
curious double ray, which gives them a strange resemblance to
a comet.

Between 1829 and 1837, Beer and Mädler made over 300
drawings of the area, and they described Messier and Pickering
as exactly alike. This is not the case to-day. Pickering is the
deeper and more distinct, and generally appears triangular,
whereas its companion is elliptical in form.

This has often been taken as evidence that change has taken
place, but as a matter of fact the 'evidence' is very slender,
because both craters show marked variations each lunation due
to the changing illumination. The writer has made at least 500
drawings of them, and has found that although Pickering
generally appears larger than Messier, it is sometimes smaller;
often the two are equal, and under high light both appear as
white spots. Walter Goodacre measured their diameters in
1932, giving a value of 8 miles for Messier and only 7 for
Pickering, despite the fact that Messier so often looks the smaller

of the pair. Probably, Beer and Mädler directed their main attention to the 'comet' rays, and it seems unlikely that any long-period change has really taken place.[1] The argument against it is strengthened by the behaviour of Beer and Feuillée, twin craterlets on the Mare Imbrium, which the writer has found to show similar alterations in apparent relative size.

However, the lunational changes in Messier and its companion are rather puzzling, and may not be due only to lighting effects. There are indications of some sort of activity round about On two occasions Klein found Messier filled with mist, which welled up from the floor and covered the western wall. Several times the writer has found both craters strangely blurred, and on August 20 1951 there was a brilliant white patch inside Pickering, so prominent that it could not possibly be overlooked. Altogether, the whole region is well worth watching.

'Mädler's square'

Closely west of the crater Fontenelle, on the border of the Mare Frigoris, Mädler drew a regular square enclosure with high mountainous walls. Neison wrote that it was "a perfect square, enclosed by long straight walls about 65 miles in length and 1 in breadth, from 250 to 300 feet in height". To-day, the enclosure is incomplete. The south-east wall, drawn definitely by both Mädler and Neison, is no longer there, but there is a conspicuous mountain mass some 20 miles south-west of Fontenelle which Mädler and Neison have considerably misplaced.

Strangely enough, the difference between Mädler's representation of the area and the modern aspect passed unnoticed for many years, and it was only in 1950 that Dr. Bartlett, of Baltimore, directed attention to it.[2] He suggested that definite change had taken place, and this led to some lively discussion between Dr. Bartlett, Professor Haas, Mr. Barcroft and the

---

[1] Dr H. Nininger, the American meteorite authority, has recently suggested that the twin craters were formed by a meteor plunging through a ridge, leaving a hole on each side. This would mean that Messier and Pickering are connected by an underground tunnel. However, this would mean a meteoric origin for the pair, which does not seem likely, as both are precisely similar in form to other craters Moreover, the 'comet' ash-rays could not be accounted for

[2] The incomplete 'square' has now been named after Dr Bartlett.

writer, from which some interesting facts emerged, as follows:

Mädler's map appeared in 1837. After a long search, the writer discovered a good photograph taken by Draper in 1863, which shows the 'square' as it is now; so that if there had been any change, it must have taken place between 1837 and 1863. Neison's book did not appear until 1876, and the fact that he still showed the complete square thirteen years after it had ceased to exist is an indication that his chart of the area is little more than a copy of Mädler's. His description can, therefore, be disregarded. This time Schröter can help us, and he seems indeed to clear up the problem. On a drawing made in 1809, the square is shown as it is at the present time, with its south-east wall missing; and, moreover, the mountain mass south-west of Fontenelle is shown in its correct position.

Why should Mädler have drawn in a definite wall? The answer is that there is a low ridge there, and the land to the west is slightly darker than that to the east, so that in a small telescope, such as Mädler used, the square looks complete. Schröter, with his larger instrument, did not fall into a similar trap. The writer has experimented with two telescopes, a small 3-inch refractor (probably almost as good as Mädler's) and a 12½-inch reflector, and has found the square much more prominent with the small instrument. With a higher power, its true nature is revealed.

Are surface changes still going on?

What is the result of all this research? We have tracked down one certain change and several possibilities; but it is true that although the lunar surface is not completely dead, alterations upon it are very few and far between. Major upheavals definitely belong to the remote past.

One thing is certain. Now that the surface has been photographed and mapped, another change such as that which destroyed the old Linné will have no chance of passing unnoticed. The face of the moon is so well known that the disappearance of a crater 6 miles across would undoubtedly be noticed; and even a smaller formation would very probably be missed if it lay, as Linné does, upon a featureless plain.

CHAPTER 12

THE OTHER SIDE OF THE MOON

OUR knowledge of the moon's surface is, of course, incomplete. The earth-turned hemisphere has been mapped very accurately, and we certainly know it better than we do the interior of Greenland, for instance. The limb zones, only well seen when the libration effects tilt them towards us, are less satisfactorily charted, but even so the main details are definite enough. Altogether, we can see some four-sevenths of the total surface. The remaining three-sevenths is absolutely unknown, and will remain so until the first explorers land upon it or an unmanned rocket equipped with a camera is sent on a circular trip round the moon to bring us back a photographic record of what lies on the far side.

The moon's slow rotation

There is no mystery about why the moon behaves in this infuriating way. Tidal friction is responsible, and there are other bodies in the solar system similarly placed. For instance, Mercury always keeps the same face to the sun, so that one hemisphere is permanently baked and the other permanently frozen –though effects similar to the librations of the moon do cause slight tilting, and there is a narrow zone, round the Mercurian equator, where the sun does appear to rise and set, always keeping close to the horizon. It is certain that the four main satellites of Jupiter always turn the same faces towards their parent planet, and probably Saturn's attendants do likewise, though they are so far away from us that it is difficult to make sure.

It is sometimes argued that the moon cannot turn on its axis at all, but this idea is clearly wrong. A simple experiment will show that we should see all sides of a non-rotating moon. Put a chair in the garden to represent the earth, and imagine yourself to be the moon. Stand behind the chair, several feet from it, and fix your eyes upon some object beyond the chair, such as a tree. Now walk in a circle round the chair, keeping your eyes fixed on the tree. When you have reached the far side of the chair, so that the tree is in front of you and the chair behind you, your back, not your face, will be pointing to the chair. To keep your face turned to the chair all the time, you must turn as you walk—in fact, you must rotate upon your axis!

Perhaps the best comment upon the lunar rotation was written some twenty years ago by a housemaid in the service of a well-known poet, and somehow handed down to posterity:

> "O moon, lovely moon with the beautiful face,
> Careering throughout the bound'ries of space,
> Whenever I see you, I think in my mind—
> Shall I ever, O ever, behold thy behind?"

Unfortunately we cannot 'behold her behind', but we can at least guess what it must be like.

What lies on the hidden side?

Conditions there are not exactly the same as those on the visible side. Day and night are unchanged, but the earth can never be seen; and owing to the difference in strength of the earth's tidal pull, the surface features may not be arranged in quite the same manner.

The trouble is that we do not know just how far the earth's tidal pull was concerned in the formation of the various surface features. Assuming that the theory outlined in Chapter 10 is more or less correct, there are two possibilities. Either the tidal strains set up had marked effects all through the period of crater formation, or else they acted merely as "the spark which set fire to the gunpowder"—in which case the crater-building processes would continue, once they had been started, until all internal activity had virtually ceased. In any case, it seems probable that there are no formations on the far side quite so vast as the Mare Imbrium, for instance. The far side may even be completely devoid of 'seas'.

This fits in well with observation, as there are no seas on the visible hemisphere which extend over the limb. The main Mare-system lies full on the disk, and the seas near the limb, such as the Mare Crisium and the Mare Humboldtianum—and, for that matter, Grimaldi—are smaller, with all their coasts visible.

There is one, the so-called Mare Incognito or 'Unknown Sea', discovered by Dr. Wilkins quite recently, which lies entirely on the far hemisphere, and so cannot be seen at all except under conditions of maximum libration; but it again is a small, complete plain, and moreover may be a mere surface sheet of lunabase, like the Mare Australe, not a true 'sea' at all.

It is also a fact that the 'frozen tidal bulge' of the moon, immediately under the earth, is marked by a large series of walled plains; the Ptolemæus chain, the Walter chain, the Clavius group, and the northern group which includes Archimedes, Aristillus and Aristoteles The disturbances in the lunar globe at the time when these were born probably resulted in parallel lines of weakness to either side, giving rise to the Petavius chain in the west (of which the Mare Crisium and the Mare Humboldtianum may both be members) and the Grimaldi chain in the east. Effects like this would probably be absent from the hidden hemisphere, and great chains of walled plains would therefore be less frequent.

The 'libration zones', parts of the far hemisphere brought into view as the moon tilts them towards us, do not tell us a great deal. Apart from the absence of large seas, they appear to be similar to the better-placed regions of the disk. There are craters of all sizes, ridges, valleys and clefts, as well as mountains and hillocks, crater-chains and 'twins'. Unfortunately, these features are not easily mapped, owing to the tremendous foreshortening. It is often impossible to distinguish between a ridge and a cleft, or a crater and a mere peak.

The libration zones in the south are particularly rough, and, in fact, contain the highest mountains known, the Leibnitz and Dörfel ranges. The Rev. T W. Webb, the great English nineteenth-century observer, was of the opinion that these ranges are merely the earth-turned walls of craters on the far hemisphere, and this suggestion has been supported recently by one of Britain's leading authorities, D. W. G. Arthur, of Wokingham; in which case the craters concerned must be huge. It is a fact that Bailly, the largest of all the normal craters that we can see, lies not far off, in the foothills of the Dörfels.

On the whole, it seems likely that the hidden side of the moon is very like the side we can see. There may be no great sea areas, but there are certainly mountains, and the usual medley of craters, ridges and clefts. In fact, the landscape is probably similar to that of the rough southern uplands of the third and fourth quadrants. However, a rather strange theory put forward almost 100 years ago by Hansen, of Denmark, is well worth mentioning.

Hansen's theory

Hansen, a famous mathematician, was engaged in investigating the movements of the moon when he found some tiny discrepancies which he could not account for. They led him to suspect that the moon was not uniform in density, but that one hemisphere was a little heavier than the other. This would result in the centre of gravity being some way from the centre of figure, and he worked out that it was actually some 33 miles further from the earth. His conclusion was that all the atmosphere and water had been drawn round to the far side, which might well be inhabited.

The theory is certainly ingenious. If it was correct, the moon would have a barren, airless earthward hemisphere, and a far side with a dense local atmosphere; the temperature there would be bearable, as the air would act as a shield against the solar rays; and the surface would be covered with vegetation, not with volcanic ash. Unfortunately, there are any number of fatal objections. Hansen's discrepancies have been satisfactorily cleared up without having to resort to lop-sidedness; the low lunar escape velocity would soon allow a dense atmosphere, even a purely local one, to leak away; an extensive air-mantle would produce obvious effects at the limb of the moon; and in any case, the effect of a displaced centre of gravity would not be to draw air and water round to one particular part of the surface. Reluctantly, we must conclude that Hansen's idea is absolutely untenable.

Rays from the hidden hemisphere

However, there is one way in which we can investigate the hidden side without resorting to rocket-cameras or space-ships. This is by studying the bright rays which come from over the limb.

There are a large number of ray-centres on the visible disk. Tycho and Copernicus are the most important, and Tycho, particularly, has scattered its ash over a vast area; but smaller systems are common enough, and there is no reason to suppose that the hidden hemisphere is devoid of them.

About eighty years ago, Dr. N. S. Shaler, an American geologist who paid a good deal of attention to the moon, began to examine the libration zones to see whether he could trace any rays which came from the far side and were not connected with any visible ray-craters. As he had expected, there were a few; and where they appeared in pairs, diverging as they passed on to the disk, it was possible to plot their tracks backwards beyond the limb, and fix the positions of the ray-centres responsible for them. Shaler plotted six centres, all well on the hidden hemisphere and thus permanently invisible from the earth.

Most unluckily, Shaler mislaid his notebooks; and when he returned to the problem, years later, he could only remember the positions of his ray-centres very roughly. Nor could he re-observe the rays, owing to the fact that his eyesight was no longer sufficiently keen. For some time, the problem was neglected, but twenty years ago a leading British observer, Dr. E. F. Emley, of Manchester, returned to it, with results very similar to Shaler's.

Dr. Emley's observations, combined with those made by Dr Wilkins and the writer, have been used by Wilkins to draw up a special limb-region section of his 300-inch lunar map, in which the rays from the far side are plotted and traced back. Eight centres are shown, at various distances beyond the limb—one, beyond the Dörfel Mountains, must be some 300 miles out of view—and three more must be regarded as probable, so that nearly a dozen formations on the invisible hemisphere have now been charted with fair certainty. Naturally, there must be errors of many miles, and it will be most interesting to find out eventually just how correct the plotted positions are.

The limb-rays are all very faint, and therefore difficult to observe. They only appear well under high light, by which time the glare from the surrounding rocks is so great that it strains the eye. This is a case where observers with small telescopes can do really useful work. As a fairly large field is essential for limb-ray searches, there is no point in using high magnification; if a low magnification is used with a large telescope, the glare becomes intolerable, so that a small instrument is best for this kind of work.[1] Photography is of no help, as no plate is capable of picking up the faint, fugitive rays among the lunar rocks.

All the evidence we can muster shows us that the hidden side of the moon is much the same as the side we can see. Great seas may be lacking, but there must be mountains and craters in plenty, along with ridges, clefts, and systems of bright rays. More than that, we cannot say at the moment. Before the first moon-voyage is accomplished, it is probable that the hidden side will have been photographed by a rocket-carried camera; but until this has been done, we shall not know just what lies beyond the towering peaks of the moon's limb.

---

[1] A tinted 'moon-glass' is worse than useless, as it completely spoils the sharpness of the image.

CHAPTER 13

ECLIPSES OF THE MOON

A TOTAL eclipse of the sun is considered a very important event. Whenever one is due, expeditions from all over the world are despatched to the most favourable site. Eclipses of the moon do not arouse nearly so much interest, and until fairly recently a total lunar eclipse was generally regarded as "spectacular, but not important". However, there are certain observations which can be carried out better during eclipses than at other times, and it is therefore wrong to regard lunar eclipses as valueless.

A solar eclipse is caused by the moon passing between sun and earth, so that the brilliant solar disk is blotted out. Nothing of the sort can happen to the moon, as there is no astronomical body between the moon and the earth; and lunar eclipses must be caused in quite a different way They are, in fact, due to the moon passing through the earth's shadow.

Cause of lunar eclipses

In Fig. 10, S represents the sun, E the earth, and MmM' the orbit of the moon. If we go into a darkened room and shine a torch upon a billiard-ball, the ball will cast a cone-shaped shadow; and as the earth, like the ball, has no light of its own, it too will cast a shadow when the sun shines on it. This shadow, shaded in the diagram, is called the 'umbra'. When the moon passes into the umbra, so that the sun, earth and moon are in a straight line, with the earth in the middle, all direct sunlight is cut off from the moon, and the bright lunar surface is dimmed.

Because the sun is a disk, and not a sharp point, the umbra is bordered by a lighter shadow-zone known as the 'penumbra', dotted in the diagram This, too, causes a dimming of the moon, although the effect is not nearly so marked.

Every scrap of direct sunlight is cut off from the moon once it passes into the umbra, but some of the solar rays will still reach it, as they are bent or 'refracted' on to it by the earth's mantle of air. One of these bent rays is shown as a dashed line in the diagram, and obviously it reaches the lunar surface, even though the moon is directly behind the earth. The result is that instead of vanishing completely, the moon turns a dull coppery colour, and can usually be found without difficulty even at mid-eclipse.

A lunar eclipse does not occur at every full moon because the lunar orbit is tilted with respect to the earth's; and for an eclipse to take place, full moon must occur exactly at a node. If full moon occurs shortly before or after the nodal point, the moon

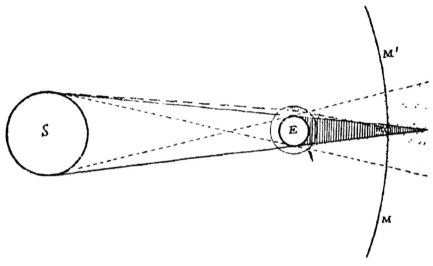

Fig. 10. ECLIPSES OF THE MOON

does not pass completely into the umbra, and we see a partial eclipse; if the distance from the node is greater, the moon misses the umbra altogether, and passes through the penumbra only. On an average, at least one umbral eclipse can be seen from any one place on the earth each year, but, of course, not all these are total. A list of forthcoming eclipses is given in the Appendix.

Fortunately, we have plenty of time to study a lunar eclipse when one does occur, as totality may go on for well over an hour. Compared with this, a solar eclipse is a very hurried affair, as totality cannot possibly last for more than seven minutes and is generally much less.

Historical eclipses

Nowadays we can predict lunar eclipses for centuries ahead, because the movements of the earth and moon are so accurately known; but as long ago as 600 B.C., Thales of Miletus, the first of the great Greek astronomers, was able to forecast eclipses with fair certainty by using a much rougher method. He knew that the sun, moon and node return to almost the same relative positions after a period of 18 years 10¼ days, the so-called 'Saros', and that consequently a solar or lunar eclipse will be followed by a very similar eclipse 18 years 10¼ days later. (This allows for five leap years in the meantime.) Naturally, the relative positions are not exactly the same, and successive eclipses not absolutely identical, but the method—first used by the old Chaldæan shepherd-astronomers—was quite accurate enough to enable Thales to predict eclipses fairly well, even though he did not know how they were caused.

Ancient ideas about eclipses were, in fact, very strange; but eventually the true cause was found. Anaxagoras of Clazomenæ, who lived about 450 B.C., certainly knew the correct explanation, and he also realized that the circular shape of the shadow showed that the earth itself must be a spherical body.

Eclipse records go back almost as far as history itself, but most of the eclipses referred to are solar ones, and the oldest lunar eclipse on record seems to have been that observed by the Chinese in 1136 B C., before Achilles and Hector fought at Troy and Homer wrote his undying *Iliad*. Two later eclipses may also be mentioned, as they too have their place in history.

In 413 B.C. the Peloponnesian War was raging; the two Greek states of Athens and Sparta were fighting for supremacy, and the Athenian army which had invaded Sicily was in serious trouble. In fact, things were so bad that Nicias, the Athenian commander, decided to evacuate the island altogether, and had he done so at once, all might have been well. Unfortunately there was a total lunar eclipse the night before the evacuation was due to take place, and the Athenians believed that it had been sent by the gods as a warning to them. The soothsayers were consulted, and advised that the army should stay where it was 'for thrice nine days'. Nothing could have suited Gylippus, the enemy commander, better. He attacked the waiting Athenian fleet, destroyed most of it and blockaded the rest in its harbour; the trapped Athenian army was utterly destroyed, and eight years later Athens herself lay at the mercy of Sparta.

The story of the 1504 eclipse is more cheerful. At that time, Christopher Columbus was in the island of Jamaica, and difficulties arose when the local inhabitants refused to supply him and his men with food. Unlike Nicias, Columbus knew a great deal about lunar eclipses, and he remembered that one was due on March 1. He therefore told the Jamaicans that unless they mended their ways he would cause the moon "to change her colour, and lose her light". The resulting eclipse so terrified the natives that they immediately elevated Columbus to the rank of a god, and the explorers had no further trouble!

Dark and bright eclipses

The effect upon the Jamaicans would probably have been even greater if the moon had disappeared completely, as has been known to happen. There were two total eclipses in 1620, the first of which was observed by Kepler, and each time the moon became totally invisible. Hevelius noted the same thing in 1642, while in 1761 the Swedish astronomer Wargentin (after whom the famous lunar plateau is named) watched an eclipse in which the moon vanished so completely that it could not be found even with a telescope, though nearby faint stars shone perfectly normally. Beer and Mädler saw a very dark eclipse in 1816, and in 1884 the shadowed moon could only just be made out.

Other eclipses are strangely bright. In 1848, for example, it was hard to tell that an eclipse was in progress at all, although the moon turned a curious shade of blood-red. Coppery is the usual hue, and occasionally there are curious reflection effects, as when the shape of Africa was clearly seen against the burnished copper disk of the eclipsed moon in 1895.[1] In April 1950 the shadow was dull grey, with here and there a tinge of reddish copper, while in January 1953 the predominant hue was coppery pink.

[1] There seem to be few accounts of this curious phenomenon, but it was clearly seen from London by a number of people.

Needless to say, these variations have nothing to do with the moon itself. They are atmospheric effects, and depend on the state of the earth's atmosphere at the time of the eclipse; it must be remembered that all rays of light reaching the eclipsed moon must pass through our air. It is probable that the tremendous explosion of Krakatoa in 1883, which scattered so much dust in the upper atmosphere that its effects were visible for years afterwards, had something to do with the darkness of the 1884 eclipse; and dust from forest fires raging in Canada caused the eclipse of September 25 1950 to be rather darker than usual.

Effects of an eclipse upon the lunar surface

To an observer on the lunar surface, an 'eclipse of the moon' would be an imposing sight. As the sun disappeared behind the earth, our world would appear as a dark disk surrounded by a glorious shining halo. However, the effect upon the moon itself would be even more striking. The solar rays are cut off as soon as the disk of the sun vanishes, and consequently a wave of bitter cold must sweep across the almost airless lunar surface. Pettit and Nicholson measured the temperatures during the 1939 eclipse, and found that they fell from 160°F. to -110°F. in the space of only an hour!

Sudden cold of this kind might well be expected to produce unusual appearances on the lunar surface, and this is one of the main reasons why lunar eclipses are now considered really interesting.

The first investigations seem to have been made some fifty years ago by Professor W. H. Pickering. He believed that some of the whitish spots on the moon were due to hoar-frost deposited during the night-time, and concluded that the spots should increase in size during an eclipse–when the cold becomes almost as great as during the night. The most prominent of these white spots is the nimbus surrounding our old friend Linné, and it is true that the patch does seem rather more conspicuous in the early lunar morning than when the sun is high above it, though the effects of contrast may be largely responsible.

Pickering and Douglass in America, and Saunder in England, made careful measurements of Linné during successive eclipses,

K

and came to the conclusion that there was definite enlargement of the white nimbus. This has been confirmed more recently, and there seems no doubt about it, even though Pickering's original idea of hoar-frost is no longer accepted.[1]

If Linné's white nimbus grows during an eclipse, some of the other white spots should behave in a similar manner; and in particular the spot near Picard in the Mare Crisium, which Birt thought to be a surface deposit, will repay close watching. The dark areas inside walled plains such as Grimaldi and Endymion may also be affected to some extent, and it is hoped that the next few eclipses will provide us with more definite information.

There is no glare from the full moon during an eclipse, and consequently occultations of stars can be particularly well seen. Unfortunately, very bright stars are seldom in the right place at the right time, and the only recorded case of a brilliant planet (Jupiter) being occulted by the totally eclipsed moon occurred as long ago as the year 755.

Finally, we come to lunar meteors. When the moon is eclipsed, the conditions for observing bright flashes in the lunar atmosphere are ideal, and the members of the Association of Lunar and Planetary Observers have indeed recorded one or two. If a bright meteor flashes across the black lunar sky during an eclipse, we may reasonably hope that it will be seen from earth by at least two observers in different positions; and then we shall have what we so badly want–positive proof of a lunar atmosphere.

A lunar eclipse may not be so exciting as a total eclipse of the sun–there are no red flames, no coronal streamers–but it cannot be denied that the passing of the moon through the dark cone of shadow thrown by our own world has a quiet fascination all its own.

[1] The writer can make no personal contribution to this discussion. He has been trying to observe lunar eclipses ever since 1934, but the English climate has defeated him every time, and he has yet to see one well from start to finish

CHAPTER 14

THE MOON AND THE EARTH

The tides

IN the far-off days when the moon and the earth were close
together, the tides raised by the two worlds upon each other
were thousands of times more violent than they are now. As
the moon drew away, the tides lessened, but even to-day, when
the separating distance has reached a quarter of a million miles,
they are still very marked.

It is certainly true that the tides are much more important to
modern man than moonlight is. We could easily do without the
friendly light which the moon sends to us–as indeed we have
to for at least a fortnight every month–but without the tides
our shipping problems would be enormously increased. Moreover, the tides provide us with a source of almost unlimited
power, though we have not yet harnessed it.

Fig. 11 will show how the tides are caused. For the sake of
simplicity, let us imagine that the entire earth is covered with
a shallow, uniform ocean. Immediately under the moon, where
the lunar gravitational pull is strongest, the waters will tend to
heap up in a bulge, and there will be another bulge on the far
side of the moon. In the diagram, M represents the moon, and
AX the earth's axis; the water-shell is shown by dashed lines,
and is, of course, drawn much larger and more elliptical than
it could possibly be in fact.

As the earth spins upon its axis, the water-heap will not move
with it, but will try to keep underneath the moon. The result is
that, as the earth rotates, the water-heaps remain more or less
stationary; the heaps pass right round the earth's surface every
revolution, and every place on the surface will have two daily
high tides.

The moon is moving in its path, so that the water-heaps
themselves are not quite still. They shift slowly, following the
moon, and on an average the high tide at any particular place
will be fifty minutes later each day. Nor will the two daily high

tides be equal. Consider a point C, which, in the diagram, has a high tide. Twelve hours later, C will have moved round to C', and will experience another high tide–but this second high tide will not be so great as the first, because the earth's axis, AX, is tilted with respect to the orbit of the moon. If the original tide is represented by CD, the second is represented by the much smaller distance C'D'. This is known as the 'diurnal inequality' in the tides.

There are other complications to be taken into account, too. When the moon is at its closest to the earth, at perigee, it naturally pulls more strongly than when it is more distant, and

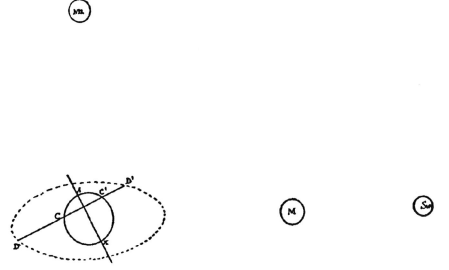

Fig. 11. THE TIDES

the tides are correspondingly higher – in fact, the difference amounts to as much as 30 per cent. Nor may the sun be disregarded. Solar tides are much weaker than those caused by the moon, but they are evident, none the less. At new or full moon, the sun and moon are pulling together, and the tides produced are strong ('spring tides'). At the first and last quarters of the moon, the sun and moon are at right angles; their pulls tend to cancel each other, and the tides are weak ('neap tides'). There will be neap tides when the moon has moved to M2 in the diagram.

As we know, the earth is not surrounded by a uniform shell of water The seas are of various shapes and depths, and consequently the tides are not nearly so simple as might appear from the figure. Local effects are very marked. At Southampton, for instance, two high tides occur in succession, as the rising water comes up two narrow straits separating the mainland from the Isle of Wight - first up the Solent, then up Spithead. Moreover, the waters take some time to heap up, and maximum tide does not therefore occur directly under the moon. There is an appreciable lag, and the highest tide follows the moon after an interval which varies according to the depth of the water concerned. Naturally, the lag is greatest for shallow coastal seas.

The moon pulls upon the solid body of the earth just as powerfully as it does upon the oceans, and 'land tides' are quite appreciable, even though we do not notice them. A rather curious fact has emerged from investigations of them. Although the solid body of the earth behaves as if it were more rigid than steel, it also proves to be perfectly 'elastic'; once the tide-raising pull is removed, the earth returns to its original shape without the slightest delay, just as an elastic band does when we stretch it and then let go.

Tidal effects are also traceable in the atmosphere. Although they are quite unimportant in the normal way, it is possible that they have some influence upon wireless transmission. Some 60 miles above the earth is a layer of 'ionized oxygen'- that is, oxygen atoms which have been damaged by the short-wave radiations from the sun, and left incomplete-and this layer, together with another 70 miles higher, makes up what is known as the 'ionosphere'. The ionosphere makes long-distance radio communication possible, as it reflects ordinary wireless waves back to the earth. (Shorter waves can pass straight through it, so there should be no trouble in establishing radio contact with the moon once we have landed there.) In 1939 Appleton and Weekes showed that the moon causes tides in the ionosphere; and more recently P. A. Howell has stated that there is a connection between lunar phases and long-distance radio reception, conditions being best about the time of full moon. However, observations of this kind are very difficult and confused, and it is not yet possible to say definitely that the moon has a measurable effect upon radio waves.

It is now believed that the earth has a metallic liquid core, some 4,000 miles across, and the suggestion has been made that tides in it have some connection with the frequency of earthquake shocks. Boneff, author of the 'tidal' theory of lunar craters, believed that a relationship between earthquakes and phases of the moon had been established, but this seems highly dubious, to say the least of it. It is true that some earthquakes occur at full moon, but the moon is full once every month- and a search for coincidences will nearly always reveal them.[1]

The moon and the weather

The moon and the weather are often linked together, but as a matter of fact there is no connection between them. Admittedly the weather does often change at new moon, but we must bear in mind that the weather changes in any case every two or three days—at least in England; other parts of the world are more predictable—and once again the 'relationship' is due to nothing more than the law of averages. An old country saying tells us that "the full moon eats up the clouds", and the sky does often clear as the full moon rises; but at the same time the sun must be setting, and the withdrawal of direct solar rays is the true cause. Thunderstorms and meteorites have also been linked with the moon, but again without the slightest justification.

However, one or two atmospheric effects are worth mentioning, even though they belong strictly to the science of meteorology and have no actual connection with the moon itself.

[1] It may be of interest to quote an example of this Early in 1952, an American radio engineer produced a paper in which he claimed to have proved that certain 'planetary configurations' had a marked influence upon wireless reception The frequency-curves he produced certainly looked most impressive, but he had been forced to bring in so many 'configurations' that it was clear he was, no doubt unintentionally, coincidence-hunting The paper was described at the British Astronomical Association in March 1952, and it was shown that the 'configurations' were even more closely related to (i) fluctuations in the light of the variable star Delta Cephei, and (ii) matinée performances of the Folies Bergère in Paris. As regards (i), the famous Delta Cephei is 600 light-years from the earth, so that the light-rays now entering our telescopes started their journey in the reign of King Edward III, and it does not seem very likely that they have much to do with the present positions of the planets in their orbits—yet the frequency curves were more or less exact. It is probably unnecessary to elaborate upon case (ii).

Blue moons

'Blue moons' are very rare, but they are seen occasionally.
J. H. Pruitt, of the United States, saw one in 1944, and A. M.
Fraser, from Queensland, another in 1949; but the best blue
moons of recent years occurred in September 1950. The writer,
observing from East Grinstead on September 26, noted: "The
moon is shining down from a slightly misty sky with a lovely
shimmering blueness – like an electric glimmer, utterly unlike
anything I have ever seen before." Many other people saw it
from various parts of the world, and blue suns were also recorded. As is always the case, dust particles in the upper atmo-
phere were responsible, due in this instance to giant forest fires
raging in Canada. The dust-pall in the New World was much
more striking. Car headlights had to be switched on at midday
in Ottawa and Buffalo, and in New York a game of baseball
was played under arc-lights.

Haloes and lunar rainbows

Haloes, or luminous rings round the lunar disk, are comparatively common, and can be really beautiful. They are not due
to dust, but are caused by moonlight catching a layer of ice-
crystals in the upper atmosphere, some 20,000 feet above the
earth. These crystals make up the kind of cloud known as
'cirrostratus'. If the cloud is lower and denser, the moon merely
looks watery. Both watery moons and haloes are said to be fore-
runners of rain, and this is true, as the cirrostratus cloud itself
often means approaching bad weather. Paraselenæ, or 'mock
moons' – brilliant images of the moon some way from the actual
disk - are also due to ice crystals, but are very rare.

When the moon shines upon raindrops in the atmosphere it
may produce a rainbow, just as the sun does, although since
moonlight is so much feebler than sunlight the lunar rainbows
are rarer, fainter and less brightly coloured. Just occasionally,
a striking one is seen. The writer, flying some 2,000 feet above
Northern Scotland on March 28 1945, was particularly fortunate; most of the rainbow circle could be seen, and even some
delicate, fugitive hues, giving a strange and lovely effect. Unfortunately, the need for navigating the aircraft did not allow
sufficient time for a proper study of the rainbow.

The 'moon illusion'

The celebrated 'moon illusion', which has been the subject of a good deal of research lately, is not an atmospheric phenomenon at all–in fact, it remains a puzzle. For some reason, the full moon appears much larger when close to the horizon than when it is higher in the sky. In fact, the ordinary observer would say that it looked about twice the size, whatever the state of the sky. Actually, the low-down full moon is slightly more distant than the high-up one, as the observer is brought towards the moon as the earth turns, and the high moon is thus a little larger than the low one–though the difference amounts to something less than 2 per cent. and is too small to be measured. Why, then, should the low moon appear so much the larger?

Ptolemy, 2,000 years ago, was well acquainted with the illusion, and explained it by saying that we automatically compare the horizon moon with nearby terrestrial objects such as trees and houses, so that it appears large by contrast. This explanation is still found in some textbooks, but it is not correct, as the illusion is still well marked when the moon rises above a perfectly featureless sea horizon. Recently, Dr. E. G. Boring, of Harvard University, has carried out experiments which indicate that the illusion is due to the behaviour of the human eye; the effort of raising the eye to look at the high moon causes the moon to shrink slightly. Whatever the cause, the illusion is in no way connected either with the moon or with the atmosphere, as people who have lost the sight of one eye–or who deliberately cover up one eye for an entire evening–are not subject to it.

The moon and plant life

Let us now consider the possible influences of the moon upon living things.

Certain small creatures undoubtedly regulate their habits by the moon; but as all these creatures are aquatic, it seems reasonable to suppose that the tides are responsible, not the moon directly. Land plants are a different matter. Fifty years ago, many farmers still believed that it was unwise to sow crops at new moon; and L. Kolisko of Stuttgart, who carried out extensive experiments between 1926 and 1935, reported a marked connection between plant growth and lunar phases. Tomatoes sown two days before full moon were said to be stronger, juicier and more tasty than those sown two days before new moon; and whereas all full-moon tomato-plants flourished, a definite proportion of the new-moon plants died. Other fruit-bearing and root crops, such as radishes, beetroots, cabbages and carrots, behaved in a similar fashion–particularly carrots, where the full-moon plants were strikingly larger than the new-moon ones. More notice might have been taken of these results but for some rather far-fetched conclusions drawn by Kolisko and her co-workers, which tended to bring discredit upon the whole series of experiments (for instance, it was maintained that the Easter full moon was particularly powerful, and had a special significance for the whole of the following year). Subsequent investigations by Rohmeder, Becker and others have not confirmed Kolisko's conclusions, and on the whole it is safe to say that even if a relationship does exist, which is most unlikely, it is of no practical importance.

Superstition and astrology

It would be a waste of time to discuss all the various superstitions which have grown up round the moon, such as the old belief that it is unlucky to see the new moon through glass; nor need we waste any space on 'astrology', the so-called science which hindered the progress of true astronomy for so many centuries. Fifty years ago, astrology was almost dead. Unfortunately, two world wars have helped to revive it, and to-day the number of practising 'astrologers' in London and New York is quite remarkable. Some of them may well be quite sincere, but it is clear that an astrologer with genuine mystical powers is about as common as a great auk. Such a doctrine, handed down to us from mediæval times, has no place in a thinking world.

Radar echoes from the moon

We have long regarded the earth and moon as closely related worlds, but only recently have we managed to make any direct contact between the two. In 1946, Z. Bay, of Hungary, made history by obtaining lunar 'echoes' of radar pulses sent out by his transmitters, and the quarter-million-mile gap between our planet and its satellite had been bridged. More extensive experiments were conducted by the United States Signal Corps and by Australian investigators, and some interesting facts emerged.

The echoes from the moon were usually clear, but the Americans reported that they sometimes faded unaccountably, and occasionally it was impossible to obtain any echoes at all for hours at a time. According to Dr. Lovell and Dr. Clegg, of the Jodrell Bank radar research station at Manchester, there are two possible reasons for this. Either varying conditions in the terrestrial ionosphere are responsible, or else different parts of the lunar surface have different powers of echo reflection. If the latter is the case, the fading may be dependent upon libration – since altering libration would cause the particularly reflective regions to shift in relative distance from the earth, causing interference and fading. Some Australian results seem to indicate that there is a connection between fading and libration, although no doubt ionospheric disturbances play an important part as well.

The radar experiments were widely publicized, and it was even suggested in the press that before long, radio methods of mapping the moon would supersede visual ones entirely. This, of course, is not the case. Radio astronomy can only support telescopic work, and can never supplant it. However, we have at least the satisfaction of knowing that the first step in bridging the abyss of space has been successfully taken.

CHAPTER 15

LIFE ON THE MOON

THE earth upon which we live is an insignificant planet, turning around an insignificant star. It is natural enough that we should regard ourselves as important, but it seems highly unlikely that our little world was singled out as the home of the only intelligent race in the Universe. (In any case, we have no right to consider ourselves as beings of a superior order. No really advanced race would allow its lands and cities to be devastated by two world wars in a single generation) There are myriads of other suns, and there are almost certainly myriads of other solar systems, so that inhabited planets are probably not so rare as we are inclined to think.

What do we mean by 'life'?

When we talk about 'life in the Universe', what we really mean is 'life as we know it', and this is an important distinction. It is within the bounds of possibility that other beings exist, made up on a pattern so strange that it would be incomprehensible to us. A friend of the writer once said that he was prepared to believe that there were intelligent beings on Mars who looked like cabbages and squeaked like mice He did not think it was probable - but it was *possible*. On the other hand, all that we know about science teaches us that our kind of life is the only kind we can understand. Once we start to consider totally alien forms, the possibilities are endless, and speculation becomes pointless, so that we have to confine ourselves to discussing life *as we know it*.

Life on other planets

Let us summarize the conditions necessary for our sort of life. There must be a reasonably even temperature, an atmosphere which contains oxygen, and a certain amount of moisture. In the solar system, there are very few worlds with all three qualifications. The giant outer planets, with their low temperatures

155

and dense ammonia-methane atmospheres, are most uninviting; Pluto is too cold; Venus has too much carbon in its atmosphere; Mercury is almost airless, and scorched on one side and perpetually frozen on the other.

Mars is the only possibility. The temperature there is bearable, and there is some moisture, as is proved by the presence of polar caps made of ice or snow. The atmosphere, though tenuous, probably contains a certain amount of both oxygen and water-vapour. Because the conditions are right, life has developed. Great darkish tracts, due to vegetation, can be seen with any small telescope. Whether any higher forms of life exist is a question so far unanswered. No earth-born creature could breathe the thin Martian air, but we can quite well imagine beings adapted to it. At present, we have no evidence either for or against the existence of advanced forms of life on Mars.

'Moon-men'

The case of Mars is a clear indication that where the conditions are suitable, life will appear. However, the moon is a much less hospitable world. The temperature-range is tremendous, and moisture is lacking. There is a tenuous atmosphere, as we have seen, but there is certainly no free oxygen, and intelligent life is therefore quite out of the question. It is rather strange to reflect that less than 200 years ago, leading atronomers were perfectly ready to believe that the moon was an earth-like world peopled with men.

The idea that the moon might be inhabited is a very old one. Indeed, once it was realized that our satellite is a cool globe it was tacitly assumed to be the dwelling-place of human beings.[1] Even the invention of the telescope did not cause a general change of opinion. It was thought that the bright areas were lands, and the dark patches true seas–sheets of open water; and although Galileo knew better, Kepler believed that the telescope had revealed a living world, with extensive oceans and a dense mantle of air.

By 1800 the idea of oceans had been abandoned, but it was

---

[1] It is not quite certain who first realized that the moon is an earth-like, non-luminous globe. Anaxagoras, friend of Pericles of Athens, certainly knew the truth as long ago as 450 B.C.

still believed that there was a certain amount of water, and that life could well survive on the surface. Schroter was of this opinion, and he was supported by the most famous astronomer of the day, Sir William Herschel.

Herschel, the Hanoverian musician who became official astronomer to King George III of England, is best remembered for his discovery of the planet Uranus, in 1781, but his main contributions to astronomy were in connection with the stars— he is justly regarded as the 'father' of stellar astronomy. Between 1781 and his death, over forty years later, every honour that the scientific world could bestow came his way. His views upon life in the solar system are, therefore, rather surprising. He thought it possible that beneath the sun's fiery surface there existed a cool region where beings could live, and he considered the habitability of the moon 'an absolute certainty'. It is on record that he once submitted a paper upon lunar mountains to the Royal Society, and before it was accepted Maskelyne, then Astronomer Royal, insisted that the paragraphs relating to lunar inhabitants should be deleted, which shows that Herschel's views were not shared by all his contemporaries.

Schröter's ideas were not so extreme, but he, too, was sure that the moon was populated. He knew that the lunar atmosphere is tenuous (a fact which Herschel does not seem to have taken into account), but he grossly over-estimated its density, and even considered that some of the formations which he observed on the moon were artificial. This idea was supported later by another German astronomer, Gruithuisen (originator of the 'meteor' theory of crater formation), who announced in 1822 that he had discovered a real 'lunar city' on the borders of the Sinus Medii, not far from the centre of the disk.

Gruithuisen was a keen-eyed observer who produced a great deal of excellent work, but unfortunately his imagination was so vivid that even in his lifetime he tended to bring ridicule upon himself. His 'lunar city' was a case in point. He described it as "a collection of dark gigantic ramparts . . . extending about 23 miles either way, and arranged on each side of a principal rampart down the centre . . . a work of art". Actually, his 'dark gigantic ramparts' turn out to be no more than low, haphazard ridges. Two of them are vaguely parallel for some distance, but there is not the slightest resemblance to an artificial structure, and in any case the ridges are so low that they cannot be identified at all except when close to the terminator. There can be no question of surface change here, as Schröter ten years before Gruithuisen, and Madler ten years afterwards, each drew the region just as it is to-day. Gruithuisen had merely let his imagination run away with him, which shows us that some of the earlier descriptions of the surface must be taken with considerable reserve

The work of Beer and Madler showed definitely that the moon is uninhabitable, at least by higher forms of life, and the moon-men were handed over to story-tellers, who have certainly used them to the full. Various strange inhabitants have been invented by various authors, but nightmarish creatures such as the tentacle Selenites of H. G Wells (in *The First Men in the Moon*) are all more or less recent. Up to the time of Schröter, Herschel and Gruithuisen, it was thought more probable that the 'Selenites' were human beings like ourselves.

The 'moon hoax'

It is, however, a fact that 120 years ago the general public was fully prepared to believe in an inhabited moon. This led to the famous 'lunar hoax', the biggest scientific practical joke of all time, which is certainly worth describing.

Sir William Herschel had explored the northern skies with his great telescopes, discovering vast numbers of double stars, clusters of nebulæ, and probing the depths of space as no other man had ever done. He found out the shape of our own star-system, and even suggested that some of the faint, misty patches of light seen in his telescopes—the spiral nebulæ—were other galaxes comparable to our own, but immensely more distant. In this he was correct, but definite proof was not forthcoming until well over 100 years later, which is a fitting testimony to his foresight. On the other hand, the southernmost stars, which never rise in the latitude of England (where Herschel made all his observations), remained comparatively unknown. Catalogues of the brighter ones had been made from time to time; Halley, the second Astronomer Royal, had actually spent the year 1677 on the island of St. Helena specially for the purpose. However, it was clear that many important objects would remain undiscovered until the southern skies were explored as thoroughly as the northern ones had now been.

It was appropriate that this task should be undertaken by John Herschel, William Herschel's son. On November 13 1833, he set out for the Cape of Good Hope, taking with him his own telescopes and equipment. He remained at the Cape for four years, and when he finally left, in 1838, his work had been well done. In fact, it took him over ten years to collect and sort all his observations.

Herschel did not intend to pay any particular attention to the moon and planets, which can be seen just as well from the northern hemisphere as from the Cape. He was mainly interested in the stars and nebulæ, and as he was breaking almost new ground there was plenty to be done. However, Richard Locke, a graceless reporter of a newspaper called the *New York Sun*, had a bright idea Herschel was on the other side of the world; communications in those days were slow and uncertain; who was there to check any statements he might care to make?

Locke saw his chance, and took it. One day, the *Sun* came out with a startling article. It stated that Herschel had modified his telescope according to an entirely new principle, and that the increased magnifying power had enabled him to discover some remarkable forms of life on the moon. After an involved description of Herschel's telescope, which would have done credit to 'Beachcomber's' famous "Dr. Strabismus of Utrecht"; the *Sun* promised its readers that further details would follow. They did. Amethyst mountains, sapphire hills and rock-columns of green basalt vied with flying unicorns, ape-men with bat-like wings, and even less probable monsters, such as "the strange amphibious creature of spherical form, which rolled with great velocity across the pebbly shore". Amazingly enough, not only the public, but also the scientific authorities were completely fooled. "These new discoveries are both probable and plausible," declared the New York *Times*, while the *New Yorker* considered that the observations "had created a new era in astronomy and science generally".

If the discoveries had been genuine, a new era would certainly have been inaugurated; and the news spread with sur-

prising swiftness. Before long the story was known all over the
world, and, incidentally, the *Sun* had more than trebled its
circulation. As soon as Herschel heard about the affair, he
naturally issued a denial; but it was more than a year before
the whole thing was definitely proved to have been a hoax from
start to finish—which goes to show that only just over a century
ago astronomers were quite ready to believe in lunar life. Taken
all in all, Locke's effort was easily the best joke ever played on
the scientific world.[1] Nowadays we are a little more realistic,
but, even so, some strange things can happen at times. In 1938
there was mass-panic in the United States when a misleading
broadcast of a play, Wells' *War of the Worlds*, led many people
to believe that the earth was being attacked by monsters from
Mars; and even more recently, since the end of the war, there
was a minor panic when an announcer on the American net-
work gave out that the moon was falling upon the earth.
Perhaps, after all, we cannot afford to laugh too loudly at our
great-grandfathers.

Pickering's 'lunar insects' \

Although the idea of intelligent life on the moon was killed
by the work of Beer and Mädler, animals and insects were
slower to die. In fact, the last serious advocate of animal life
upon the lunar surface was not Wells, Verne or any other story-
teller, but a very famous astronomer--Professor W. H. Pickering, author of the 1904 photographic atlas and a vast number
of papers concerned with all branches of lunar study.

Between 1919 and 1924 Pickering, observing from the clear
skies of the island of Jamaica, carried out a detailed study of
the noble crater Eratosthenes, which forms the southern termination of the Apennine chain. He found a number of strange

[1] Its only rival is the 'comet-seeker' hoax of 1891, of which Professor Barnard,
the famous observer of comets, was the victim One day, a San Francisco paper,
the *Examiner*, came out with an article which stated that Barnard had invented
a telescope which would discover comets all by itself, ringing a bell when it had
found one¹ The article had obviously been written by an astronomer, and was
so ingeniously worded that it sounded almost plausible. Barnard immediately
wrote a frantic disclaimer to the *Examiner* and all other San Francisco news-
papers, and was horrified to find that not one of them would publish it, with the
result that for the next two years he received letters from all over the world
asking for further details of his remarkable instrument. The author of the hoax
was never definitely tracked down, although everything pointed to Barnard's
friend and colleague Professor Keeler, later Director of the Lick Observatory.

LIFE ON THE MOON

dark patches which showed regular variations each lunar 'day'; and although he was perfectly sure that vegetation tracts did exist on the moon, he suggested that the Eratosthenes patches, which moved about and did not merely 'spread', were better explained by swarms of insects.

This startling idea was put forward in Pickering's final paper on the subject, published in 1924. He pointed out that a lunar astronomer of a century ago would have seen similar moving patches on the plains of North America (due to herds of buffalo), and the Eratosthenes patches were about this size, though they moved more slowly—only a few feet a minute—and it was therefore reasonable to assume that the individual creatures making them up were smaller than buffalo. Although insects were considered the most likely answer, Pickering's paper contains the following remarkable paragraph:

"While this suggestion of a round of lunar life may seem a little fanciful, and the evidence on which it is founded frail, yet it is based strictly on the analogy of the migration of the fur-bearing seals of the Pribiloff Islands. . . . The distance involved is about twenty miles, and is completed in twelve days. This involves an average speed of six feet a minute, which, as we have seen, implies small animals."

Pickering's idea was that the creatures, animal or insect, travelled regularly between their breeding-grounds and the dark 'vegetation tracts' nearby. His reputation ensured that due attention would be paid to the theory, but nowadays it is not taken at all seriously. The supposed creatures would have to put up with a total lack of water, an equal lack of oxygen, and a daytime temperature of over 200° F. Also, they would appear to be extraordinarily regular in their habits, moving almost to the nearest hour. In any case, Pickering's 'moving patches' have never been properly confirmed, although there is no doubt that the colour of the surface in the region does alter with the rising sun; and it is most unlikely that his 'feeding grounds' are really vegetation areas. In fact, there are so many objections to the theory that it can only be described as fantastic. Like Grui-thuisen's city and Locke's bat-men, lunar insects must be relegated to the world of fiction

L

Possible plant life

Plants remain to be considered, and here we must be much more cautious. Admittedly, the conditions on the moon are uncomfortable, and any vegetation would necessarily be of a very low type; trees and bushes are certainly out of the question, and even grass is too advanced. If plants exist, they must be of the lichen or moss type, and they must survive precariously in a few favoured localities on the surface.

From a botanical point of view there are no insuperable objections to the idea, provided that we admit a very tenuous atmosphere with a ground density of rather less than 1/10,000 of our own. Plants can live in curious places. For instance, the Antarctic lichens of our own world do very well in districts where the temperature never rises more than a degree or two above freezing, and is nearly always far below; other plants manage on a vanishingly small supply of oxygen and moisture, and we know that vegetation is abundant on Mars, despite the thin and oxygen-poor atmosphere. Naturally, no terrestrial organisms could possibly survive if transferred to the moon, but it is not impossible for something of the lichen or moss type to exist upon the bleak lunar surface.

There are a number of craters which show definite and more or less regular variations each lunation. Most, such as Endymion, Grimaldi and Riccioli, have darkish lunabase floors. Endymion contains patches which are greyer than the general tone of the floor, and alter in shape as the sun rises over them; some expand, others contract and even vanish. Pickering was convinced that vegetation was responsible; and although it is now more generally believed that the patches are due to the solar heat affecting something unusual in the surface coating, causing it to change in hue, the question is still very open.

Another crater to which Pickering devoted a great deal of attention was Aristillus, on the Mare Imbrium, some way east of the Caucasus Mountains. Here he detected two strange parallel streaks which developed with increasing solar heat, and which he called 'canals'–a most unfortunate name, since it implies artificial construction, and no such idea was in Pickering's mind. The Aristillus streaks are certainly perplexing, but not nearly so interesting as the radial bands inside Aristarchus, the brilliant crater on the Oceanus Procellarum which can justly be regarded as the most remarkable object on the entire moon.

The radial bands of Aristarchus

Even when it is illuminated by nothing more powerful than the earthshine, Aristarchus can often be seen glowing almost like a star, and its central peak is definitely the brightest point upon the lunar surface. The great Herodotus Valley lies nearby, and it was in this area, too, that Wood's ultra-violet photographs led him to the discovery of sulphury deposits; bluish hues have been reported periodically during the last 150 years, and there are also undeniable mists. Yet in form Aristarchus is normal enough. It is 23 miles in diameter, with walls rising to 6,000 feet above the floor, and the glittering central peak is not of exceptional height. It is the interior details which are so unusual.

As soon as the sun has risen sufficiently for the east wall of Aristarchus to be free from shadow, very faint dark shadings are seen upon it. As the lunar morning progresses, and the crater-floor emerges from the bitter blackness of night, the shadings darken, and are seen to be really parts of well-defined bands, which radiate from the central mountain, cross the floor, and run up the inner slopes of the walls. They develop steadily, and by midday the most prominent of them often pass right over the wall-crest and on to the outer country. In moderate-sized telescopes they appear continuous; but using the Meudon refractor in 1952, Dr. Wilkins and the writer found that the main bands could be resolved into series of dots and dashes. This appearance, similar to that found by Antoniadi, the celebrated Greek planetary observer–using the same telescope -for the canals of Mars, cannot be seen except with a very large instrument. As the sun sinks, and the temperature drops, the bands become less conspicuous; and by the time they become engulfed in the evening shadows, they are hard to make out at all.

Nowadays the main bands are glaringly obvious with even a small telescope, and yet the earlier observers overlooked them altogether. Beer and Mädler, who examined Aristarchus very carefully, made no mention of them; neither did Löhrmann, and an early Schmidt drawing, which shows Aristarchus on a large scale, also omits them.

The bands were first described by Phillips in 1868 (though a drawing made five years before by Lord Rosse, using his great 72-inch telescope at Birr Castle, in Ireland, shows them unmistakably), but his observations do not seem to have become widely known. Neison's book contains a long description of Aristarchus, but makes no mention of the bands, and nothing more was heard of them until 1884, when Sheldon recorded two. Since then, they have been growing gradually more and more conspicuous, and the latest charts show eight or nine. Moreover, they are not structureless. They originate on the crater-floor, some way from the base of the central mountain, in darkish 'bulbs', and each band is made up of a dark centre bordered on either side by a greyish streak. Bright points are often seen on the crater-walls between two band areas.

Robert Barker, who has spent many years studying the moon and is one of Britain's leading authorities, has carried out a thorough investigation of the problem, and has come to the conclusion that the bands have definitely become more prominent during the last eighty years. It is indeed hard to see how Schröter, Mädler, Löhrmann and Schmidt could all have overlooked them if they had been as conspicuous then as now, particularly as all four observers paid great attention to Aristarchus and drew it frequently under all conditions of lighting.

Other banded craters

For many years the bands of Aristarchus were considered unique, but during the last twenty years many smaller craters have been found to possess similar systems. A good example is Birt, an 11-mile crater close to the Straight Wall, shown in Plate III. There is also Moore, east of Bullialdus on the Mare Nubium, where the writer detected bands in 1949 while drawing the nearby cleft system. Over two dozen smaller banded craters are now known. Like the hill-top craters and the domes, they are commoner than has been believed, and have not been listed before simply because no serious search for them has been made. It is significant, however, that Aristarchus is the only large crater to show radial bands.

What are the bands?

Several explanations have been put forward to account for these curious markings. It was even suggested that they had no real existence, and were due to tricks of the light. It is perfectly true that they are most often seen on the eastern walls of craters, opposite to the sun; but as the eastern wall is always the first illuminated in the lunar morning, the bands develop most rapidly there. In any case, the Aristarchus bands, which are typical of all the rest, are much too prominent to be dismissed as illusions. It is also worth recording that Thornton has recently detected a band in the small crater Dionysius, near the Ariadæus cleft, which runs to the north wall, and is therefore not directly opposite the rising sun.

It is possible that the bands are lava flows, smoother than the bright surroundings and therefore comparatively dark under high light. An electronic origin has also been suggested. However, neither of these theories can explain the gradual development of the bands, and it is clear that the bands darken slowly from their bases to the tops of the crater-walls as the day progresses.

In 1951, A. P. Lenham, of Swindon, who has made a close study of the banded craters, put forward an explanation which is ingenious, if not entirely convincing. He suggested that the bands are formed by clusters of crystals, which during the night-time absorb moisture oozing from the ground. During the day, the temperature is so high that the vapour evaporates; the crystals lose their water and become dark. Unfortunately it is difficult to believe that bands composed of clusters of crystals would be so regular as the observed bands actually are, and moisture is unlikely to exist in quantities great enough to make Lenham's process possible. Moreover, the gradual extension of the bands is as great a difficulty as it is to the lava flow theory.

In 1951 the writer suggested a different explanation. It is highly speculative, and perhaps based upon rather slender evidence, but it may perhaps be worth a certain amount of consideration.

Let us imagine that after almost all activity had ceased in Aristarchus, there was a final explosion from the central mountain - perhaps the eruption which scattered ash-rays across the surrounding plain -and the almost hard floor cracked radially from the centre. The crater was then left with a system of narrow radiating clefts, very delicate and deep. The mists still visible from time to time prove that a certain amount of internal activity still persists, and it is suggested that this activity causes tenuous vapour to leak out of the radial cracks- only during the daytime, during the night, any vapour is frozen solid.

As the sun rises and warms the cracks, the gas begins to escape, and a very primitive vegetation, which has been lying dormant throughout the bitter night, seizes hold of it and begins to develop. This goes on until the temperature starts to fall again, when the vegetation dies down. At last, the evening shadows cause all local atmosphere to freeze, and the plants become dormant again, remaining so until they are awakened by the next sunrise.

This would account for the gradual spread of the bands away from their bases. Most gas would still be emitted from the region of the central mountain, which is still the centre of activity, and the vegetation would therefore develop most quickly in this area. The band structure, a central strip with a more diffuse border of thinning vegetation, would also be expected. The occasional mists no doubt mark outbursts of more violent activity, and a general increase over the past sixty years may be responsible for the increased prominence of the bands. If so, the increase is probably temporary.

Of course, there are a great many objections to this theory. No clefts have ever been seen in the positions of the bands, but this can be accounted for by the fact that by the time the sun has risen sufficiently for details to be well examined, the bands have already developed enough to hide any delicate surface cracks. Many of the smaller band-craters, even those of the size of Birt and Moore, have no central peaks, though this is no bar to a late convulsion of the surface having taken place.

The emitted gas is certainly not oxygen or water-vapour, and we can only guess as to its nature; but carbon dioxide, which is a heavy gas and, incidentally, the last manifestation of dying volcanic activity, seems a likely answer.

Undoubtedly the lunar vegetation, if it exists, is very different from anything we find upon the earth; but it does seem probable that if there is any living thing upon the lunar surface, it is to be found inside Aristarchus and other craters of similar type.

What, then, have we found out about lunar life?

We have found that the 'moon-men' of countless story-tellers cannot exist; that animals and insects are also out of the question; and that terrestrial-type plants are certainly absent. On the whole moon there is no living thing, apart perhaps from a few scattered patches of lichen or moss-type vegetation on the floors of some of the craters.

Past life on the moon?

Speculations about past life on the moon are rather point-less, because we know so little about the history of our companion world. If current theories are right, the moon turned from a fiery mass into a globe shaken by tremendous activity, and finally into an inert world, comparatively quickly on the astronomical time-scale. The atmosphere, always unsuitable for breathing, leaked away; and by the time the earth was cool enough to support aquatic life, the moon had changed from a raging inferno into a silent, almost airless planet. Therefore, it does not look as though higher forms of life could ever have developed. For one thing, the conditions were never right; for another, there was no time. It took earth-creatures some 1,000 million years to develop from primæval seaweeds and shell-fish into apes and men, and the whole history of lunar activity, from the 'molten' to the 'modern' stage, was probably run through in less time than this. Low forms of plants are as much as could ever have been expected.

Throughout its existence, then, the moon has been a barren world. No beings have scrambled across the surface rocks; no footsteps have echoed on the plains, and no eyes have ever beheld the wonders of the lunar sky. Now, after countless ages, a new era is at hand; and in a few more ticks of the cosmic clock, the landing of the first men from another planet will bring life at last to the silent, waiting moon.

CHAPTER 16

THE WAY TO THE MOON

Voyages to the moon

THE idea of space-travel is by no means new. It goes right back to the ancient Greeks, and as long ago as the year A.D. 160 we find Lucian of Samos describing an imaginary trip to the moon. Ever since then, lunar voyages have been discussed at regular intervals; but so long as our own atmosphere remained unconquered, space-flight was bound to remain nothing more than a dream of the far future. Now that we can fly at will in the air, we are quickly learning how to make interplanetary travel a real possibility. With united research carried out upon a peaceful earth, we could probably reach the moon within twenty years; with the situation as it is, it may take at least fifty.

There seems little doubt that we shall eventually be able to explore the whole solar system, from tiny Mercury to frozen Pluto-though all these worlds, apart from Mars and Venus and one or two of the larger satellites, seem to be most inhospitable, and probably unsuitable for actual landing. For the moment, however, there is only one body under serious consideration, and that is the moon. The distance is comparatively very small – remember that the moon is 100 times as close as Venus, nearest of the planets – and although sheer distance is not so important as might be thought at first sight, many of the main problems are simplified when we do not have to wander too far from the earth. We shall learn so much from the first few lunar voyages that the longer journeys, to Venus and Mars, should present very few extra hazards.

The airlessness of space

In any case, what are the main difficulties in the way of interplanetary travel?

To start with, there is no air in space. This is not a great disadvantage in itself. We can take our own air with us, and there would be no difficulty in doing so, particularly as we need not worry about the nitrogen, which makes up three-quarters of our normal atmosphere but is not actually of any use to us. What we need is oxygen, and this could easily be stored in our space-craft. It is safe to do without the diluting nitrogen for long periods, if not indefinitely, and we need have no fear of choking through lack of air.

The vacuum of space does, however, mean that none of our ordinary flying machines will work there. Balloons, for example, depend on air density, while an aeroplane obtains its lift by means of the disturbance in the air caused by its propeller, and buoys itself up by its wings. In a vacuum, the propeller would have nothing to 'grip on', and the wings would be useless. (In any case, normal motors need to draw upon the oxygen in the atmosphere.) Since the war, we have reached the 'ceiling' of ordinary flight; even the high-altitude aircraft now made are limited to heights of something like 10 miles. They cannot rise higher, because there is not enough air to give them lift.

Ten miles may seem a long way, but it is not much in comparison with the distance to the moon. If we represent the earth by a globe 55 yards in diameter, the moon will shrink to a 14-yard globe about a mile away. The mantle of effective atmosphere will then be reduced to a ring round the earth rather less than 3 inches deep. There is thus no chance of "building up speed in the air by means of propellers, and then coasting for the rest of the distance", as was suggested by one story-teller.

The pull of the earth

It is in fact the earth's gravitational pull which is the main obstacle in the way of space-flight. If we could neutralize it in some way, most of our troubles would be over. Unfortunately, we cannot. H. G. Wells, in his famous story *The First Men in the Moon*, invented ' cavorite', a substance which cut off gravity from everything above it; but one of Wells' many gifts was that he could present a scientific impossibility in a convincing way. With him, the story came first and science afterwards; and he knew perfectly well that his 'cavorite' went against all the laws of Nature. It is quite certain that anti-gravity material of this type is out of the question, and so we have to put up with the constant drag of our own world.

If we start our space-ship off with a jerk at escape velocity, 7 miles a second, we can leave the earth behind without any further application of power. If we start at a lower speed, we shall have to keep on applying power for much of the journey; and, as will be shown later on, this would mean using so much fuel that no space-ship could hope to carry enough It is clear, then, that we must reach escape velocity, by building up to it in the earliest stages of our journey. Once escape velocity has been reached, all power can be cut off, and the rest of the journey accomplished in what is known as 'free fall'.

Fuel, then, is a great problem. The atomic motor may solve it completely, but at the moment our knowledge of the atom is comparatively small, and it would be most unwise to base our hopes upon the prospect of 'tapping' a source of almost unlimited power. At present we pin our main hopes on the rocket motor; but before considering the problem as we see it to-day, let us see what past writers had to suggest as methods of transport.

The space-gun

We can at once dismiss the authors who evaded the issue by introducing supernatural agencies, and also those who made use of obvious impossibilities such as waterspouts (Lucian of Samos) and bird-power (Godwin, who published a book in 1638 in which his hero trained gansas, or wild swans, to tow him through the air on a raft—only to find out later that they hibernated on the moon, and were taking him with them) The space-gun, though equally impossible so far as manned projectiles are concerned, has a scientific basis, and is chiefly remembered owing to the famous story by Jules Verne, *From the Earth to the Moon*. Verne believed in accuracy, and a good many details of his space-gun are correct; but unfortunately he overlooked two all-important facts. No human being could stand up to the sudden jerk of being fired from a gun at 7 miles a second, and in any case the tremendous air-resistance would destroy the projectile before it had even left the barrel. As a matter of fact, Verne must have realized that rockets will work in a vacuum, as he used them later on in his story; and it is rather surprising that he did not use rocket power for the whole trip. On the whole, his space-ship was not so good a forecast as his submarine, which he described with amazing accuracy long before anything comparable had been built or even planned.

There is another objection to the space-gun idea. Short of building another gun on the moon, there could be no return, and such a prospect would be rather too bleak for real-life adventurers. It is possible, however, that space-guns may eventually be used for firing non-manned projectiles away from airless worlds with low escape velocities.

Verne overcame the return journey difficulty by introducing a wandering asteroid, which pulled the projectile out of its course, swung it round the moon and returned it to earth. As a matter of fact, however, it is unlikely that any asteroids do lie in the region between the earth and the moon; we should have found them by now. The tiny asteroid Hermes was comparatively conspicuous when it passed us by in 1938, though it was twice as distant as the moon and is not much more than a mile in diameter. If we do have a second satellite, it can only be a few yards across. (In passing, it may be mentioned that Pickering once carried out a photographic search for a body revolving round the moon—a satellite of a satellite!—but without success.)

The principle of the rocket

Aeroplanes, anti-gravity and space-guns having failed us, we come back to the rocket; and here we find much more encouraging prospects. To appreciate the position fully, we must make sure that we understand the way in which a rocket works.

Imagine a sleigh lying on perfectly frictionless ice. If I stand on one end of the sleigh and jump off, the sleigh will move one way and I will move another—because, as Newton pointed out, "every action has an equal and opposite reaction" (Fig. 12). If I weigh the same amount as the sleigh, we shall move at equal speed; if not, the lighter body will go the faster. If the sleigh has twice my weight, it will start off with half my speed. Note that this would be so whether there was any surrounding atmosphere or not. 'Reaction' is responsible, and air has nothing whatever to do with it.

Now consider the simplest form of rocket, which consists of

a tube filled with explosive, and with a hole or 'exhaust' at one end. When the explosive is fired, the generated gases try to expand in all directions. They can only do so in one direction— where the hole is—and so they rush out of the exhaust. Just as my kick moved the sleigh, so the 'kick' of the gases moves the tube; and the faster the gases rush out, the greater the movement imparted to the tube. Speed, in fact, depends on exhaust velocity. A stick added to the tube, to give it stability, turns it into a rocket of the kind all of us have fired on Guy Fawkes' night

Here again, the movement of the rocket would take place just as well in vacuum as in air. The rocket moves because of

Fig 12. THE PRINCIPLE OF REACTION

the reaction to the ejection of gases from the exhaust; and so far from being a help, the atmosphere is actually a hindrance— because of air resistance. Clearly, then, a rocket will be at its best in interplanetary void.

So far as is known, rockets were invented by the Chinese about the year 1200, and were (of course) used as weapons of war. In 1232, a rocket barrage was actually employed against the Mongolians. Five and a half centuries later, Hyder Ali of Mysore used a similar but more effective barrage against the British at Guntoor, and this led an army officer, Colonel Congreve, to make a full investigation of the military possibilities of the rocket. He did succeed in interesting the Government, but developments in artillery made the rocket obsolete very quickly, and it was hardly used in war again until our own time. As a matter of fact, the rocket is neither accurate nor efficient at low speeds and low altitudes. Rocket cars were in the news twenty years ago, and one of the early pioneers, Max Valier, killed himself experimenting with them; but they were never satisfactory. Rocket postal services likewise proved erratic, and the only real use for the rocket so far has been at sea, where it has been of great value in carrying rescue lines to ships in trouble.

At high altitudes, the rocket comes into its own, and as early as 1908 Dr. Robert Goddard, of the United States, realized that it could be used for carrying scientific recording instruments out beyond the atmosphere. His preliminary results appeared eleven years later. Undoubtedly his ultimate objective was the moon, but he did not say so definitely in his published booklet, and the first men to explore the possibilities of space-travel by rocket were Ziolkovsky, of Russia, and Esnault-Pelterie, of France. The idea was developed by Professor Hermann Oberth, of Roumania, who laid the foundations of the future science of 'astronautics' in two books, one published in 1923 and the other in 1929. In 1927 the first of the world's Interplanetary Societies was formed, in Germany, and the dawn of the new age was at hand.

Liquid-fuel rockets

The word 'rocket' is apt to conjure up a picture of a firework racing a few hundred feet into the air, and then exploding in a blaze of coloured sparks. Early rockets were of this type, but it soon became obvious that solid fuels, such as gunpowder, were of no use for space-travel. They are not controllable, and they weigh too much, besides being relatively inefficient. The German experimenters turned their attention to liquid fuels, and Goddard, working independently along the same lines, actually fired the first liquid-fuel rocket in history on March 16, 1926.

Naturally, Goddard's rocket was a comparatively complex affair. Instead of being a mere powder-filled tube, it had to have a firing chamber for the burning to take place; pumps; ignition mechanism; and storage tanks for the liquid oxygen and whatever else was used (petrol, for Goddard's original rocket). The 'rocket' was obsolete, and the 'rocket motor' had been born.

Gradually, interest was kindled all over the world, even in Great Britain; but it was too much to hope that the 'astronauts' would be left to continue their experiments unhampered. The politicians stepped in. The official view was that rockets might well be useful, but that the idea of space-travel must become of secondary importance to the more vital task of wiping out hundreds upon thousands of men, women and children. The same Governments that had sneered at the original experimenters were soon pouring millions of marks, dollars and pounds into perfecting the rocket as a weapon of destruction. Von Braun, one of the rocket pioneers who later worked at the Nazi research station at Peenemunde, is credited with the remark: "Oh, yes, we shall reach the moon but of course you mustn't tell Hitler that!"–and Germany was by no means the only offender. The attitude of statesmen towards rocketry is another proof, if one were needed, that human knowledge has outstripped intellect.

Despite the unworthy motives behind it, military research did enable the new science of astronautics to make great strides. First the German V2s, and later American rockets, soared high above the effective atmosphere; and if we go back to our old scale, with a mile between the earth and the moon, we have now covered 6 feet (only with unmanned rockets, admittedly). This may not seem much, but it must be remembered that the 'first few yards' of the voyage are certain to be much the most difficult. Once the rocket is in free fall, the journey will become more or less uneventful up to the moment of landing.

However, it soon became clear that no single rocket could possibly work up enough speed to free itself from the earth. The highest exhaust velocities yet obtained are in the region of 2 miles a second, and to carry one man to the moon on this basis (neglecting the weight of the space-ship altogether) would need some 30 tons of fuel. In the future, higher exhaust velocities will certainly be obtained, and the situation will improve; but all the same, it has been shown that it will never be possible to send an ordinary rocket direct from the earth to the moon, using chemical fuels only.

Step-rockets

This might seem to be a death-blow to the whole idea of space-travel, but fortunately it is nothing of the kind, as Dr. Goddard realized at a very early stage in his experiments. The problem can be solved by the 'step-rocket'.

Late in February 1949 a German-type high-altitude rocket took off from White Sands, the leading rocket research station of the United States, carrying an unusual load -not an explosive charge or a camera, but a smaller rocket. As it reached the top of its climb, the large rocket dropped away and fell back to earth, while the small one commenced firing and continued its journey. The small rocket therefore began its own flight with a considerable initial height and speed; moreover it was above the worst of the atmosphere, so that it was able to reach a record altitude of some 250 miles This is the principle of the step-rocket. There is no need to confine ourselves to two steps only, and using sufficient steps we can theoretically reach any desired speed, although the engineering problems of multi-step rockets are extremely complicated.

If the first lunar space-ship does take off direct from the earth's surface, it will therefore be a step-rocket, carrying enough fuel to allow it to take off again from the moon on its return flight. Fortunately, taking off from the moon is comparatively simple, owing to the lesser escape velocity and the lack of air resistance (the tenuous lunar atmosphere is far too thin to make itself felt). Let us examine some of the main experiences we are likely to have.

Effects of weightlessness

During the short period while the rocket is accelerating to escape velocity, the travellers will be subjected to great pressure; they will have to lie down, and they will not be able to move at all easily This will only last for a minute or two; and as soon as the rockets cease firing, all sensation of weight will vanish. It was here that Jules Verne, accurate though he usually was, made a mistake. In his 'projectile', which was in free fall–just as the space-ship will be–he made his travellers weightless only at the point where the gravitational pulls of the earth and moon exactly balance, some 24,000 miles from the moon.[1] It is true that the terrestrial pull is preponderant on the earthward side of this point, and the lunar pull on the moonward side; but the pull on the travellers, and indeed on everything else inside the ship, is equally strong, so that the travellers are in free fall just as much as the ship is - and therefore weightless. A parachutist jumping out of an aeroplane is in free fall, and so feels no weight until he pulls his rip-cord (air resistance being neglected). It is not strictly true to say that our normal feeling of weight is due to gravity. More properly, it is due to our resisting the pull of gravity, which is trying to draw us down to the centre of the earth. Out in space, in free fall, we are not resisting anything and so we shall not feel any weight until the rockets are switched on again, to slow us down preparatory to landing.

It will take us some time to get used to the conditions of zero gravity. We turn a glass of water upside-down, and not a drop comes out; we hold a pencil in front of us and let it go, and it remains suspended in the air. An ordinary fountain-pen, which relies on gravity to draw its ink downwards, will not work. Our muscles are just as strong as they are when we are in the earth's grip, and sudden movements are therefore dangerous, as they will result in painful bumps against the cabin walls. Moreover, every non-fixed article will start moving, slowly but surely, once it is touched. A book pushed to one side will take off and wander gently across the cabin, until it rebounds from the opposite wall. Everything not in actual use will have to be fixed, otherwise the whole space-ship will be in a state of constant chaos.

As is always the case with a new venture, many people have shown that there are fatal objections to the whole idea. (Remember that Professor Simon Newcomb, an eminent American scientist, proved conclusively as late as 1902 that flying in a heavier-than-air machine was absolutely impossible.) It has been said, for instance, that the human body will not stand up to conditions of zero gravity. Actually, there seem to be no grounds for anticipating any trouble on this score. The most essential

---

[1] In any case, the so-called 'neutral point' is a myth. The pull of the sun there is just as effective as it is at any other point on the earth-moon trip.

organ, the heart, does not depend upon gravity; and apart from a possible loss of balance, due to the disturbance of the mechanism of the inner ear, it is unlikely that any discomfort will be felt. The writer well remembers coming across a boy leaning against a wall and standing on his head, eating a bun. He explained that he wanted to see whether it was possible to swallow upwards, and the fact that he was able to do so easily may not be without its significance.

In any case, artificial gravity can be created if we set the whole space-ship spinning. This would not be a difficult matter, but all the indications are that it will not be necessary.

Meteors are also held to be a source of grave danger, but here again the risks have been magnified out of all proportion. Meteors large enough to do real damage are extremely rare, and the chances of a space-ship being fatally damaged on the lunar voyage are rather less than one in 10,000. Even if the hull was punctured, the air would not rush out in the fraction of a second, as has often been supposed. Unless the hole was really large, the crew would have plenty of time to repair it before enough oxygen had leaked away to make them lose consciousness.

Another objection raised is "the bitter cold of space". Actually, space is a vacuum, and can have no temperature at all. A blackened surface exposed to the sun would absorb a considerable amount of warmth, and ordinarily enough heat could be obtained from the sun to make the inside of the space-craft perfectly comfortable, though heaters would naturally be carried for use in an emergency.

Landing on the moon

Landing techniques are likely to be very complicated, and at the moment we can do no more than touch on them. Air-braking can be used on the return journey to earth, but on the almost airless moon all such methods are useless. The only solution, therefore, is to rotate the space-ship until its rockets point to the moon, and at the critical moment fire one or more of them until the speed has dropped so much that a gentle landing can be made. A feeling of weight will return to the

M

travellers as soon as the first 'brake-rocket' is fired, and the odd effects of zero gravity–the water that will not pour out, the book that moves, the pencil that floats–will vanish.

The space-station

Very possibly, the first lunar voyage will be made in a step-rocket of this sort, but it is clear that escaping from the powerful pull of the earth is not going to be easy. We cannot neutralize it, and the only alternative is to take off from somewhere else. Suppose we could start our lunar voyage from a base situated in space, thousands of miles above the earth's surface?

The idea of an artificial space-station may sound fantastic, and so it would be if we had to devise some means of keeping it up. But the real situation is very difficult. The key to it is that an artificial station set in the right orbit, outside the limits of the atmosphere (or, more correctly, at a height where the atmospheric density has fallen off so much that air resistance has become negligible), will not fall back to the earth, but will continue circling indefinitely. It will, in fact, become an independent satellite.

If a stone is fastened to the end of a string and whirled round, it will not drop. It will keep circling, and the string will remain taut as long as the stone is whirled quickly enough. The shorter the string, the faster we must whirl it to keep the stone from falling. Gravity acts in much the same way. For instance, little Mercury, close to the sun, speeds along at 30 miles a second, whereas remote Pluto is content with a leisurely two and a half miles a second. If Pluto quickened up to Mercury's velocity, it would fly off at a tangent and leave the solar system altogether. If Mercury was reduced to Pluto's crawl, it would spiral into the sun. Consequently, an artificial satellite nearer to us than the moon is would have to move more quickly, relative to the earth, than the moon does.

There are two great differences between our whirling stone and the whirling space-station. First, the stone is spinning comparatively slowly in a powerful gravitational field acting in one direction only; and secondly, it is being braked all the time by air resistance. Neither of these factors are operative for a station beyond the atmosphere. Once the station has started revolving steadily around the earth, what is there to stop it doing so indefinitely? Nothing.

Of course, it is hopeless to build an artificial satellite on the earth and then try to fire it into a circular orbit above the atmosphere. The only possible method is to build the station actually out in space.

The first step will be to send a rocket into a circular orbit well beyond the limits of the effective atmosphere. If a 'sideways' thrust is applied at the right moment, the rocket will settle into a permanent orbit, and will become the nucleus of the future station. Others will be sent up to join it, and the station will be assembled by crews wearing space-suits, propelling themselves by gas-jets or miniature rocket motors.

The problem of making a rendezvous with a rocket circling round the earth at a tremendous speed may sound difficult, but is not actually so. It must be remembered that this speed is only the speed relative to the earth. If a second rocket joins the first in its orbit, the two will be stationary relative to each other. There is some analogy to two motor-cyclists riding abreast, but a better one is to consider the earth and moon themselves. Both are whirling round the sun at 18 miles a second, but, as we have seen, there is no chance of their flying apart and separating for ever.

As both the first and second rockets would be in the same orbit, there would be no sensation of relative speed, any more than there is in a conventional aeroplane flying straight and level at a height of 2,000 or 3,000 feet. Nothing would have any weight,[1] as everything would be in free fall, and a single man could easily handle a mass which would weigh many tons on earth. Gradually, a complete space-station could be built up. The rays of the sun could be used as a source of heat; the outer hull would be airtight, so that the crews would be able to dispense with their space-suits when inside the station itself. If necessary, artificial gravity could be introduced. The station will probably be disk-shaped, and if it was rotated nine to ten times a minute the gravity on the edge would be much the same as that which we are used to, though it would fall off to

[1] Theoretically there would be a certain amount of 'weight' due to the mass of the space-station itself, but this would be completely negligible. The earth's pull would not be felt at all, due to the station's orbital velocity.

zero at the centre of the station. Once the disk had been set in rotation, it would continue to spin indefinitely – because there would be nothing to stop it.

The first space-stations will certainly be built fairly close to the earth. Perhaps 500 miles above the surface is the lowest limit. The later stations, true 'space-cities', will be much more remote. A station set up at a distance of 22,000 miles would go round the earth once a day, so that it would appear fixed in our sky – just as the earth does as seen from the moon, though for a different reason.

The uses of an artificial satellite as a laboratory, observatory, radio and television relay station and in many other ways are so obvious that it is unnecessary to stress them; but perhaps the station's main use will be to serve as a 'jumping-off' base for the moon and planets. Starting from the station, we have no need to work up to an escape velocity of 7 miles a second. Not only are we so far from the earth that terrestrial gravity is greatly weakened, but we can make use of our own natural orbital velocity; and all we have to do is to increase our speed from 'circular velocity' to 'escape velocity', which presents no difficulties at all.

Space-ships of the future

Rather regretfully, we have to realize that the cylindrical, streamlined space-ship of the story-books will have to be abandoned. Admittedly, the ferry-rockets between earth and space-station will have a winged stage for use in the atmosphere; but wings and streamlining are quite useless in space, where there is no air, and on the moon, where there is only a trace. The future space-ship is much more likely to be a sphere, or, if atomic motors are used, two spheres joined by an arm – one ball containing the crew-rooms, and the other the dangerously radio-active motors. A craft of this type would never land on the earth. It would be built in space, and it would spend all its life in space.

Whichever comes first – the space-station or the lunar rocket – we can no longer consider the moon unreachable. Terrestrial 'isolationism' was killed on the day when Dr. Goddard launched his first liquid-fuel rocket. Unless a third world war throws civilization back to the Stone Age, we should get to the moon while some of those pioneers who worked on the early rockets still live. Let us hope that the first expedition will be made not by Britain, by America or by Russia, but by representatives of a United Earth. Before we can claim to be masters of inter-, planetary space, we must learn to be masters of ourselves.

CHAPTER 17

THE LUNAR BASE

IT would be very half-hearted to visit the moon once or twice, and then leave it once more to its unending silence and desolation. Moreover, the moon has for us an importance which we can only dimly realize as yet; and if we are going to colonize it, as seems probable, the first step must be to make refuelling possible either on the moon itself, or on a satellite station revolving round it. On the whole, the former alternative sounds the more attractive. The disadvantages surrounding take-off from the earth do not apply to the moon, where the escape velocity is comparatively low and there is no air resistance to worry about Clearly, then, we must construct a lunar base.

Establishing a permanent base

Although the first journey to the moon should be made before the end of the century, we cannot yet tell how soon it will be possible to establish a permanent base there. Much depends upon the way in which space-flight is accomplished. If it begins as a direct earth-moon trip, there will be no chance of transporting much material for the construction of a base; and without a permanent structure, no man will be able to stay on the lunar surface for any length of time. Space-suits are likely to be uncomfortable things. If an artificial satellite already exists in an orbit some thousands of miles from the earth, the situation will be much brighter, and it will be possible to land all kinds of materials upon the lunar surface.

It is pointless to go into details about the choice of an initial site, but there are various 'essentials'. The first base will certainly be built on the earth-turned hemisphere, probably not very far from the apparent centre of the disk, and it will be in comparatively smooth country. The Mare Imbrium seems particularly suitable, but it must be remembered that we have no knowledge about local conditions. The pioneers may well find that the surface structure is far better in another place.

The humble beginnings of the base will be isolated pressurized huts, but as soon as possible it is obviously desirable to have a large enclosure provided with air and protected from the extremes of temperature outside. The most likely form is a large dome, made of some strong and preferably transparent substance. A plastic dome, inflated to normal terrestrial atmospheric pressure, would need no additional support; in fact, it would be a huge air-bubble on the moon, with a tough outer skin, and a system of air-locks for entering and leaving

Obviously, it would be bad policy to have one dome only. Accidents will happen, and we cannot altogether disregard meteorites, for instance, even though the lunar atmosphere seems to afford adequate protection. Any puncturing of the dome, or failure of air supply, would force the colonists to take emergency action; and it would certainly be advisable to allow for a quick evacuation of all those not actually needed into a completely independent dome.

With regard to the actual dome, we are reduced to pure speculation, because we do not know how much material can be brought from the earth – nor do we know definitely what useful substances are likely to exist on the moon. All the work will have to be done by men wearing space-suits; and on the whole, the task will be almost as difficult as that of building an artificial satellite. In a circular orbit, there is no weight except that due to the growing space-station itself, which would be absolutely negligible, while on the moon gravity can by no means be disregarded, though it is only one-sixth of what we are used to. It must be remembered, too, that inertia is unaltered; and though it would be surprisingly easy to pick up an axe on the moon, it would be no easier to swing it than would be the case on the earth- because the axe still has its original mass.

The space-suit

Moreover, the space-suit is not going to be the simple affair that many people imagine. Fiction-writers equip their heroes with tough, flexible suits and helmets, and then assure us that there will be no difficulty in moving about. Unfortunately they forget that on the moon there is no outside pressure; and consequently a suit of this sort would not be able to stand up to the strain. It would simply spread-eagle the wearer, and make him feel most unhappy. The usual pictures of space-suits, reminding one of a diver's outfit, are most misleading. There is no analogy; under the sea, all the pressure is from the outside, and serious difficulties do not arise.

The space-unit will therefore have to be rigid, and may end up by being a cylinder with motor-driven legs (or wheels) and mechanical arms. It is certainly unlikely to be comfortable. Air supply presents no special problems, but temperature control does. On the moon there is a tremendous difference between sunlight and shadow, and the space-unit will therefore have to be an efficient insulating unit against both heat and cold. The inside heat, generated by the wearer's body, may then become a serious menace, and altogether there are many problems connected with space-suits which remain to be worked out. On Mars, where the atmosphere is reasonably dense, the 'diver' type of suit may be adequate; but it is definitely unsuitable for use on the moon.

Transport and communications

Transport will be another minor problem. In the far-distant future, when domes have risen on the moon in large numbers, railways may be extensively used. Ordinary wheeled vehicles would hardly be usable on the rough lunar surface (caterpillar treads would be better), and no terrestrial-type flying machines could be employed, owing to the lack of air. The rocket is not a good answer so far as short-range transport is concerned, since nothing will make it efficient at low speeds.

There is also the question of communication. It will be easy to keep in touch with the earth, as we can use wavelengths to which the terrestrial ionosphere is no barrier; but, strange to say, it will be extremely difficult to use wireless on the moon itself, except over very short distances. Ordinary radios, such as those carried in space-suits, will be limited to about 2 miles–the distance of the horizon. A 100-foot mast would increase the range to something like 12 miles, but even this is inconveniently limited, and it is not easy to see just what can be done. As the earth's ionosphere lies some 60 miles up, and the lunar atmosphere has an equal density at an equivalent height, it is of course within the bounds of possibility that the moon has an ionosphere; and if this is so, the problem will solve itself. We must hope for the best. Incidentally, we do not know whether our compasses will work. The moon may or may not have a magnetic pole. Very probably it has, but we have no idea of either its position or its strength.

Solar radiations

Another function of the earth's atmosphere is to shield us from certain harmful solar rays of short wavelength, which are absorbed in the upper air. Here again the lunar atmosphere may do something to help, but as yet there is no way of finding out definitely. The dangers from ultra-violet rays are undoubtedly real, and if the moon's air-mantle does not screen us it will be necessary to take special precautions. Once again, we must simply wait and see.

Life in the lunar base

Let us now see what help the moon itself is likely to give us when we start constructing our permanent base. There is no reason to suppose that useful minerals are lacking in the lunar rocks. Whether or not the moon was formed from the earth, it is probably composed of the same fundamental surface substances, and we may be able to mine most of the materials we need. It will be particularly important to find out whether there are any available substances which can be used as rocket propellents. One of the chief advantages of the lunar base will be that it will allow us to refuel on the moon, and it is obviously more economical to manufacture fuel on the spot than to transport it a quarter of a million miles from the earth.

Food is a different matter. It is possible, as we have seen, that very low forms of plant life may exist in certain places, but they will certainly be useless for eating,[1] and it is unlikely that we shall be able to persuade any terrestrial-type plant to adapt itself to the rigorous lunar conditions. When there is enough

[1] The writer cannot help conjuring up the harrowing picture of a starving lunar prospector staggering down the inner slopes of Aristarchus in the vain hope of finding a lichen or two. It is not a pleasant prospect!

space inside the 'air-bubble', food can be grown; but for the first few years everything will have to be brought from the home planet, and the colonists will have to get used to a rather unappetizing diet of concentrates. Soilless or 'hydroponic' farming, in which the plants are placed on netting and fed by means of liquids circulating underneath, may help to some extent.

Uses of the lunar base

There are always people who do their best to ridicule and decry any new venture. One can well imagine their attitude towards colonizing the moon. "What's the use?" they will ask. "Why trouble to go to another world, when there is so much of our own left uncultivated? What will be gained, even if we do manage to set up a permanent base there?"

Doubtless Columbus, Livingstone and Amundsen had to put up with this sort of question before they set out on their immortal journeys. It may be true that it would be easier to set up a permanent base in Antarctica than on the moon, but a little thought shows that the lunar base will bring us many benefits.

For one thing, laboratories and observatories will be set up under conditions which we can never approach on earth. Astronomy will benefit particularly. Terrestrial telescopes are severely handicapped by the turbulence of our atmosphere, and on the moon a comparatively small instrument would show as much as the 200-inch reflector does from the top of Mount Palomar. A really large telescope erected on the lunar surface would, indeed, open up the universe for our inspection.

Medicine would also benefit It is known that some diseases, particularly those affecting the heart, might be checked by reducing the pull of gravity, and experiments on the moon (as well as on satellite stations) will tell us more about this. In the far future, some hundreds of years ahead, there may well be a lunar dome which is nothing less than a huge hospital.

One more of the many uses of the base may be mentioned. It will provide a stepping-stone to the planets. It is relatively easy to break free from the moon; and even if satellite stations have been constructed by then, the first voyages to Venus and Mars may start from the lunar surface. If the lunar base comes before the satellite station, the travellers will take off from the earth, land on the moon, refuel, and then take off again for another planet.

All this shows us that the lunar base is certain to be of real benefit to humanity. Even if not, it is safe to say that we should still want to go to the moon. Alexander the Great sighed for new lands to conquer, and we are all Alexanders at heart; the spirit of adventure still lives in us.

At the present time, the nations of the world are uneasy. War-talk is in the air, and a third senseless orgy of self-destruction, which would destroy all that is good and noble in the human race, is still a possibility. A common purpose, a common objective, might well end all the hatred that has been deliberately fostered between the different races of our own planet and if statesmen could be persuaded to forget their own personal ambitions, and band together in some great enterprise mankind might enter upon a true 'golden age'. Interplanetary travel provides us with the perfect objective. We know that i can be accomplished, and we know that it will be accomplished the only question is–"When?" In a hundred years' time, wil the moon shine down from the star-studded night sky upon warring earth, still tantalizing, still mysterious and still un conquered?

We must do our best to see that this does not happen. At al events, men will one day land upon the moon. The pioneers o to-day call across the years to the explorers of tomorrow "Good luck!"

CONCLUSION

IN this book, we have travelled a quarter of a million miles in space and perhaps 500 years in time. Since Stone Age men gazed at the glowing lunar disk, and wondered whether the moon was a god or the abode of a god, we have learned much. Four-sevenths of the moon's face is well known; we know the conditions we are likely to meet when we land, and we know too that the old, depressing picture of a dead and totally airless globe is a long way from the truth. I have tried to give my readers a true picture. If I have failed, the fault lies with me, and not with the Queen of Night.

Finally, let me anticipate a question often asked me: "Why do you spend so much time gazing at the moon through a telescope? What is the use of it?" The answer should be clear. If I want to visit a foreign country, I do not merely pack a suitcase and jump on board the first aeroplane. If I have never been there before, and have no idea of what I am going to find, I buy a travellers' guide-book. What we are trying to do at the moment is to draw up a travellers' guide-book for the moon; and even if the men of 1953 are never able to use it—well, in the years to come, other people will.

APPENDIX A

OBSERVING THE MOON

IT is often believed that useful astronomical work can be done only at a great observatory, and that in consequence the modestly equipped amateur is wasting his time. So far as the moon is concerned, nothing could be further from the truth. It is true that the amateur's scope is limited, but really valuable work can be accomplished. Comparatively delicate detail can be seen without the use of very high powers, and provided that observations are carefully and intelligently made (which is not always the case!) the results are well worth while. Remember that Mädler, perhaps the greatest of all nineteenth-century lunar observers, never had anything larger than a 3¾-inch refractor until after he had more or less abandoned lunar work altogether.

The favourite instrument for the beginner is a 3-inch refractor, and this is probably the smallest telescope with which serious observations can be made. The refractor employs a lens or 'object-glass' to collect its light, and the image produced is then magnified by a second lens known as the 'eyepiece'; the reflecting telescope has no object-glass, but collects its light by means of a mirror. In the usual type of reflector, the Newtonian, the light passes down an open tube (which may be a skeleton) and falls on to a mirror, which is shaped so as to reflect the light-rays back up the tube and concentrate them on to a smaller mirror, or 'flat', near the upper end. The flat is inclined at an angle, and reflects the beam of light into the side of the tube, where it is brought to focus and the image magnified by the usual eyepiece.

Both types of telescope have their own advantages and drawbacks. The reflector is more trouble; mirrors need periodical attention. On the other hand, it is both handier and cheaper.[1]

[1] Note that the aperture of a telescope, usually given in inches, indicates the diameter of the object-glass (for a refractor) or main mirror (for a reflector), and inch for inch the refractor is much the more powerful. A 6-inch refractor, for instance, is much superior to a 6-inch reflector; and although a 3-inch refractor is large enough for serious work, a 3-inch reflector would not be of much use.

A clock-drive, which allows for the rotation of the earth and keeps the moon (or whatever is being observed) in the field of view, is very convenient, but certainly not essential. The writer's 12½-inch reflector is not equipped with one, but has 'manual slow motions', i.e. rods which can be twisted to shift the telescope very slightly. The result is perfectly satisfactory. Even slow motions are not necessary for a smaller instrument, and for a 3-inch refractor they are probably more trouble than they are worth.

Mounting, however, is vitally important. Small refractors are often sold on table 'pillar and claw' stands, which look very nice, but are about as steady as blancmanges. The best answer is a tripod, and a converted wooden camera tripod will do quite well, provided that it is heavy enough. For anything more than a 6-inch, something rather more permanent - such as a concrete pillar - is desirable.

Town-dwellers are at a grave disadvantage compared with those more fortunate people who live in the country. Railway stations, smoking chimneys and street-lights are no help to astronomers, and this is why the Greenwich Observatory is at present being moved from its old site to the remote peacefulness of Herstmonceux, in Sussex. Smoke and lights have to be tolerated, but the fatal thing is to try to observe through a window. Apart from the difficulty of keeping the telescope rigid, the temperature difference between the room and the outer air causes so much local atmospheric turbulence that the moon generally appears as though shining through several layers of water. Sharpness of image is essential, and it can never be obtained from indoors.

Neither is it much good trying to observe a low moon, as the light then reaching the observer is shining through a thick layer of unsteady atmosphere. Twilight, however, is no handicap; the glare is reduced, and very good views are often obtained against a fairly light sky. Neither is slight mist harmful in the normal way, though even the thinnest layer of cloud is always fatal. Often a very brilliant starlight night (such as occurs after heavy rain) will prove hopelessly unsteady, with the moon's limb shimmering and rippling, and under such conditions there is nothing to be done except to stop observing.

Beginners often make the mistake of using too high a power. On a really good night, of course, it is possible to use high magnifications to advantage; but it is no good using a powerful eyepiece unless the image obtained is really sharp. Whenever a lower power will do equally well, it should be used. The writer worked entirely with a 3-inch refractor for some ten years, and found that a power of 100 diameters was usually adequate. 130 could often be used, and just occasionally as much as 250, but powers over 200 were only used on excellent nights to 'finish off' drawings which were already more or less complete. Dr. Wilkins generally employs between 300 and 400 on his 15½-inch reflector, and on the writer's 12½-inch reflector 330 is the best power for general use, though higher magnifications can of course be employed when necessary. We found that powers of about 300 on the 33-inch Meudon refractor and the 25-inch Newall refractor at Cambridge University showed much delicate detail that had not found its way into the maps. The great apertures of these telescopes provided such resolving power that very delicate details could be seen even without very high magnification. Pure magnification, in fact, is by no means the most important factor. Steadiness and good definition are much more vital in the long run.

The general procedure to be recommended for making a lunar drawing is as follows:

First, select the formation to be drawn. Survey it, and decide just what area is to be covered. Then, using a fairly low power, sketch in the main outlines (unless they have been prepared beforehand from a previous drawing or, preferably, a photograph). Also indicate the shadows and coarser details. Then change to a higher power, and insert the finer details. If the night is really good, maximum possible magnification should be used to check each tiny feature, but details which are doubtful or suspected only should be clearly marked as such- on the whole, it is better to make a written note of doubtful objects than to put them in the actual drawing.

Some observers make their 'final' drawings actually at the telescope. Others, less artistically gifted (such as the writer!) make comparatively crude, though accurate, drawings at the telescope, and then transfer them neatly into an observing book.

It is, however, most important to enter the 'fair copy' immediately on leaving the telescope. The temptation to 'leave it till to-morrow' will almost certainly result in mistakes in interpretation. If possible, the completed drawing should be checked again at the telescope to make sure that no errors have crept in. This may seem a lengthy procedure; but one really good drawing is worth a hundred fairly good ones.

When the drawing is complete, the following data should be added: year, date, time (using the 24-hour clock, and never Summer Time), telescope, magnification, name of observer, position of the terminator, and any other relevant information, such as observing conditions. If any of this is missing, the value of the drawing will be drastically reduced.

Another common fault is that of using too small a scale, which involves drawing too large an area at once. Twenty miles to the inch is a convenient scale, and it is better to be over-generous than parsimonious. A small-scale, cramped drawing is of no possible use, as small details cannot be recorded. Some time ago, the writer was sent a drawing of the complete Mare Imbrium, made with a 5-inch refractor, in which the Mare Imbrium was about 4 inches across and Plato perhaps a centimetre. Even if the drawing had been accurate (which it was not) it would still have been valueless.

Drawings are of two main types, line drawings and shaded sketches. (Shadows should always be shown.) The drawings in this book made by Mr. Ball and Dr. Wilkins belong, of course, to the latter class; a line drawing, by the writer, is shown here (Fig. 13). Despite the difference in appearance, an indifferent artist is recommended to keep mainly to line drawings, which can be made just as accurate, even though they are much less spectacular.

Desultory and aimless sketches of lunar features are not really of much value, and the amateur who intends to do something useful should set himself a definite programme–perhaps an observing list of about a dozen interesting formations. Drawings of these should then be obtained whenever possible. The most impressive views will, of course, be had when the object is near the terminator, but if the observing list contains formations scattered all over the moon there are bound to be one or two suitably placed at any set time. Moreover, it is not true to say that high-light drawings are of no value. The reverse is the case, particularly with the dark variable areas such as the floors of Endymion and Grimaldi.

There are many formations on the moon, and to learn the names of even the main ones takes a certain amount of time

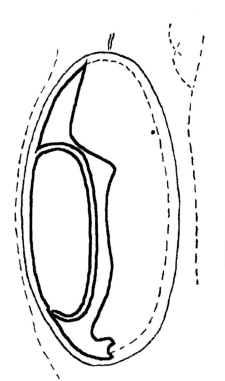

Ingalls, a small crater close to Riccioli and formerly known as Riccioli C, was sketched by the writer on April 8 1952 It has no central height, but the floor contains a complete ring. The shape of the shadow shows that the wall-height is decidedly uneven.

Fig. 13. THE CRATER INGALLS

Apr 8, 1952, 22h. 20m 33 in. O G. (Observatory of Meudon). × 250.
Co-long. 77° 7. (Patrick Moore, F R A.S)

and patience; but even if no conscious effort is made to memorize them, it will be found that the chief features will be recognized in a very short time. The writer, who started serious lunar observing in 1937 with a 3-inch refractor, adopted a definite system. In a large observing book, each named formation was allotted a separate page, and within two years a drawing of each formation had been secured – rough in many cases, but

N

enough to enable the object to be recognized again without difficulty. The trouble taken proved worth while, and saved a good deal of time in the end.

Naturally, a map is essential. The outline given in this book is on a very small scale, and can be used only to identify the main features. Some reliable maps are listed in Appendix B.

Next, what useful work can be done by the amateur with a small telescope?

It would not at first seem that much could be gained by making a drawing of a well-placed formation, such as Ptolemæus. Large telescopes will pick up details far beyond the beginner's range. On the other hand, there is always the chance of picking up something new. The writer well remembers detecting a new system of dark radial bands while drawing clefts near the crater concerned. He was only drawing the clefts because he was comparatively unfamiliar with them, and had not the slightest idea of looking for anything new.

Near the limb, where details are not at all well mapped as yet, the small telescope comes into its own. Most of the classical maps are of no help, because they are drawn to mean libration. An instance of this may be given. In the outline map on page 193 there is a large crater, Scott, shown near the south pole of the moon, in the region of the Leibnitz Mountains. It is right on the limb, but under good libration conditions it moves on to the disk, and another large formation, Amundsen, appears behind it. Amundsen cannot be shown on the outline map, because under average conditions of libration it cannot be seen at all. Only Wilkins' map gives a special libratory section, and much work remains to be done in charting the very foreshortened details. A 3-inch is capable of showing much that is not on any of the maps.

Of course, it is necessary to choose one's time for this work. Not only must the limb formation under study be well placed with regard to libration, but it must also be on or near the terminator—otherwise it will be so obscure that it will probably not be found at all. Moreover, each limb-sketch must be positively identified. A vague note such as 'south-east limb' is not enough. A named crater should preferably be included in each sketch, so that the area can be fixed without any chance of error.

No two drawings of any area will be alike, no matter how good the observer. Lighting changes cause tremendous alterations in appearance. If a limb region is to be studied, it should be drawn as often as possible over several lunations, and the drawings then combined into a reliable and comprehensive chart.

Rays, unlike other formations, are best observed under high light, and here a small telescope is just as effective as a large one. High magnifications are not normally needed, and a low power used on a large telescope means a great deal of glare. (Tinted eyepiece-caps known as 'moon-glasses' are sometimes used, but in the writer's opinion all they do is to wreck the definition.) No really reliable ray-chart has yet been constructed; and although some ray-centres on the hidden hemisphere have been tracked down, there are certainly many more waiting to be discovered. The amateur can do valuable work here.

It is clear, then, that lunar studies are within the range of even the very modestly equipped observer. The moon is full of surprises, and the owner of a 3-inch telescope will find more than enough to occupy him, provided that he possesses the two essential qualities of an amateur astronomer–enthusiasm and perseverance.

APPENDIX B

LUNAR LITERATURE AND
LUNAR MAPS

SOME references should be made to lunar literature. These notes are in no way complete; all that has been done is to select some books and maps of obvious value. Many of them are now out of print, but most can be borrowed from the various astronomical libraries.

Neison's *Moon* (Longmans, Green and Co., London, 1876), the first of the English classics, is now difficult to obtain, but copies of it are to be found now and then. It contains Neison's map, really a revision of Mädler's, and a detailed description of each formation named on it.

Elger's *Moon* (Geo. Philip and Son, London, 1895) is also out of print. This is unfortunate, as his map is very clear and his concise description of the lunar surface most valuable. However, the map has been revised by Dr. Wilkins and re-issued, so that it can now be easily obtained.

R. A. Proctor's *Moon* (Alfred Bros., Manchester, 1873) is concerned mainly with the motions of the moon, and remains probably the best introduction to this branch of lunar study. It is not difficult to get.

Nasmyth and Carpenter's *Moon* was published some seventy years ago by John Murray's, of London. It ran to several editions, and copies of it are still about. It was written mainly to advance the 'volcanic fountain' theory, but is well worth studying, and some of Nasmyth's photographs of his lunar models are beautiful.

W. H. Pickering's photographic atlas of the moon (Annals of Harvard College Observatory, 1904) has the advantage of showing each area of the surface under five different conditions of illumination, which no other photographic atlas does; and in conjunction with an outline map such as Elger's, it makes crater recognition very easy.

Goodacre's map of 1910 is out of print, and the same unfortunately applies to his book, *The Moon*, privately published in 1930. However, a reduced copy of the map was included in the general astronomical work, *Splendour of the Heavens*, written by various authors (Goodacre himself wrote the chapter on the moon), and produced in 1923.

R. B. Baldwin's *Face of the Moon* (University of Chicago Press, 1949) is concerned largely with the meteoric theory of crater formation, but nevertheless contains a vast amount of miscellaneous lunar information.

J. E. Spurr's three books, *Features of the Moon, Lunar Catastrophic History* and *The Shrunken Moon* (Lancaster Press, Pennsylvania, 1944-9), are devoted to his volcanic theory, and are intended only for the serious student.

Dr. H. P. Wilkins is at present preparing a book which will contain his 300-inch map, on a reduced scale, and a complete description of the surface (in which the present writer is collaborating). It is hoped to finish this by the summer of 1953.

As well as these books, there are the various observatory and society publications. The British Astronomical Association, founded in 1890, has its headquarters in London; eleven Memoirs of its Lunar Section have appeared, and the last three are still in print, while copies of the earlier ones are not too scarce. They contain a vast amount of information, and lunar notes are also scattered through the sixty-two volumes of the Association's monthly Journal. The Association of Lunar and Planetary Observers, founded since the war by Professor W. H. Haas, has its headquarters in Las Cruces, New Mexico, and issues a monthly journal, the *Strolling Astronomer*; this, too, contains a tremendous amount of information about all aspects of lunar study.

APPENDIX C

FORTHCOMING LUNAR ECLIPSES

THE following list of future eclipses may be found useful. The first four columns need no explanation. The fifth column, headed 'Mag.', is the magnitude of the eclipse, 1·0 or greater being total, anything less than 1·0 partial. For instance, 0·5 means that the earth's shadow reaches half-way across the moon at mid-eclipse. Column 6 gives the geographical longitude and latitude where the moon is overhead at mid-eclipse. Columns 7 and 8 indicate whether the eclipse can be seen from England or from the United States. 'Partly' may indicate that the whole eclipse may be visible, but very low in the sky, or that the moon rises or sets while the eclipse is in progress.

Year	Month	Day	Time, U/T (Mid-eclipse) h m		Mag.	Moon overhead Long	Lat.	Visible in England	U.S.A.
1953	Jan.	29	23	50	1 3	6 E	18 N	Yes	Partly
,,	July	26	12	19	1 9	177 E	19 S.	No	Partly
1954	Jan	19	2	34	1 1	36 W	21 N.	Yes	Yes
,,	July	16	0	22	0 4	4 W.	22 S	Yes	Partly
1955	Nov	29	17	6	0 1	101 E	21 N.	Partly	No
1956	May	24	15	31	1 0	126 E	21 S.	No	No
,,	Nov.	18	6	47	1 3	105 W	19 N	Yes	Partly
1957	May	13	22	32	1 3	21 E	18 S	Partly	No
,,	Nov.	7	14	28	1 0	139 E.	16 N.	No	Partly
1958	May	3	12	11	0·03	176 E	16 S.	No	Partly
1959	Mar.	24	20	17	0 3	57 E	2 S.	Partly	No
1960	Mar.	13	8	30	1 5	125 W	3 N	No	Yes
,,	Sept.	5	11	23	1·4	171 W.	7 S.	No	Partly
1961	Mar.	2	13	32	0·8	160 E	7 N	No	Partly
,,	Aug.	26	3	8	1 0	46 W	11 S	Partly	Partly
1963	July	6	22	0	0 7	31 E	22 S	Yes	No
,,	Dec.	30	11	7	1 4	166 W	23 N.	No	Partly
1964	June	25	1	7	1 6	16 W.	23 S	Yes	Partly
,,	Dec.	19	2	35	1·2	40 W.	23 N.	Yes	Yes
1965	June	14	1	51	0·2	28 W.	23 S	Yes	Partly
1967	April	24	12	7	1 3	178 E.	13 S	No	Partly
,,	Oct	18	10	16	1 1	158 W.	10 N.	No	Partly

Year	Month	Day	Time, U/T (Mid-eclipse)		Mag.	Moon overhead		Visible in:	
			h	m.		Long.	Lat.	England	U.S.A.
1968	April	13	4	49	1 1	72 W.	8 S.	Partly	Yes
,,	Oct	6	11	41	1·2	178 W.	5 N.	No	Partly
1970	Feb.	21	8	31	0 05	124 W.	11 N.	No	Yes
,,	Aug	17	3	25	0 4	50 W	14 S	Partly	Yes
1971	Feb.	10	7	42	1 3	112 W	14 N.	Partly	Yes
,,	Aug.	6	19	44	1·7	65 E.	17 S.	Partly	Yes
1972	Jan.	30	10	53	1 1	160 W.	18 N.	No	Yes
,,	July	26	7	18	0 6	108 W.	20 S	No	Yes
1973	Dec.	10	1	48	0 1	29 W.	23 N.	Yes	Yes
1974	June	4	22	14	0 8	26 E.	22 S.	Yes	No
,,	Nov.	29	15	16	1 3	128 E.	21 N.	No	No
1975	May	25	5	46	1 5	87 W.	21 S	No	Yes
,,	Nov.	18	22	24	1 1	20 E.	19 N.	Yes	Partly
1976	May	13	19	50	0 1	62 E	18 S.	Partly	No
1977	April	4	4	21	0 2	64 W.	6 S	Partly	Yes
1978	Mar.	24	16	25	1·5	115 E.	2 S.	No	No
,,	Sept.	16	19	3	1·3	73 E.	3 S.	Partly	No
1979	Mar.	13	21	10	0·9	45 E	3 N	Yes	No
,,	Sept	6	10	54	1 1	164 W.	7 S.	No	Partly
1981	July	17	4	48	0 6	71 W	21 S	Partly	Yes
1982	Jan.	9	19	56	1 4	63 E.	22 N.	Yes	No
,,	July	6	7	30	1·7	112 W	23 S.	No	Yes
,,	Dec.	30	11	26	1 2	171 W.	23 N	No	Yes
1983	June	25	8	25	0 3	126 W.	23 S.	No	Yes
1985	May	4	19	57	1·2	60 E.	16 S.	Partly	No
,,	Oct.	28	17	43	1 1	90 E.	13 N	Partly	No
1986	April	24	12	44	1 2	168 E.	13 S	No	Partly
,,	Oct	17	19	19	1 3	67 E.	10 N.	Yes	No
1987	Oct.	7	3	59	0 01	63 W.	5 N.	Yes	Yes

APPENDIX D

DESCRIPTION OF THE SURFACE

(All formations mentioned here are shown in the outline map.)

First (north-west) quadrant

THIS quadrant contains two major seas (Mare Serenitatis and Mare Crisium) and most of another (Mare Tranquillitatis), together with nearly all the Mare Vaporum and parts of the Mare Frigoris and the Mare Fœcunditatis. There are many interesting objects, including the great cleft systems associated with Hyginus, Ariadæus and Triesnecker; and the great Alpine Valley, as well as Linné, the most-studied formation on the entire surface. The chief mountain ranges are the Caucasus, the Hæmus and the western Alps.

ARAGO. An 18-mile crater on the Mare Tranquillitatis, with a low central hill. There are two low domes close by, one to the north of Arago and the other to the east.

ARCHYTAS. A fine bright crater on the north coast of the Mare Frigoris, 21 miles across and 5,000 feet deep. There is a central peak.

ARGÆUS. This and ACHERUSIA are the two capes on either side of the strait separating the Mare Serenitatis from the Mare Tranquillitatis. Argæus is the higher of the two, and casts a fine, pointed shadow at sunrise.

ARIADÆUS. A 9-mile crater in the highlands separating the Mare Tranquillitatis from the Mare Vaporum, connected with the great cleft first seen by Schröter in 1792. The cleft, over 170 miles long, runs out on to the Mare Vaporum, cutting through several shallow rings in its path; in places it is blocked by rocky débris, and branches from it connect with those from the Hyginus crater-cleft. The Ariadæus cleft can be seen with a very small telescope when suitably placed.

ARISTILLUS. A fine bright crater on the western part of the Mare Imbrium, 35 miles across, with high terraced walls rising to 11,000 feet above the floor. The walls are very brilliant at times, and there is a central peak. Pickering thought that the dark streaks seen under high light, extending from the centre westwards on to the outer plain, were due to vegetation.

ARISTOTELES. A very conspicuous walled plain, 60 miles across and 11,000 feet deep, on the southern border of the Mare Frigoris. There is a central hill-group. Very closely outside Aristoteles, to the west, is a smaller and shallower formation, MITCHELL.

ATLAS. A magnificent 55-mile crater not far from the darkfloored Endymion. Atlas' much-terraced walls rise to 11,000 feet above an interior which includes much detail—one or two old rings, some delicate clefts, crater-pits, and dark patches which show regular variations each lunation.

AUTOLYCUS. The companion to Aristillus. Autolycus is 24 miles across, with terraced walls 9,000 feet above the floor. There is a central mountain.

BESSEL. The most conspicuous crater on the Mare Serenitatis. Bessel is 12 miles across, with bright walls. A prominent bright ray passes through or very near it, and to the west lies the conspicuous Serpentine Ridge.

BOSCOVITCH. A curious formation on the Mare Vaporum, 27 miles in diameter, with low walls and a very dark floor.

BURG. A 28-mile crater between Atlas and Aristoteles, with a large central peak. Closely east of Bürg lies an ancient plain crossed by a large number of clefts, some of which can be seen with a very small telescope.

CASSINI. On the western area of the Mare Imbrium known as the Palus Nebularum (Marsh of Mists). Cassini is a curious shallow formation, 36 miles in diameter. In it is the small crater A, which in turn contains the WASHBOWL.

CAUCASUS MOUNTAINS. An important range dividing the Mare Serenitatis from the Mare Imbrium. Some of the peaks rise to 12,000 feet.

CHALLIS. The southern member of a pair of 'twins' very close to the North Pole (the other is MAIN). Challis is some 36 miles in diameter, and the wall between it and Main is barely traceable.

CLEOMEDES. A magnificent walled plain 78 miles in diameter, closely north of Mare Crisium. There is a mountain in it nearly, though not quite, central; and the dark interior contains much detail. The walls, which rise to 16,000 feet, are broken in the north-east by a very deep crater, TRALLES.

CONDORCET. A fine regular crater 45 miles across, on the border of the Mare Crisium. North of it are two smaller and less conspicuous craters, HANSEN and ALHAZEN–the latter not, of course, identical with the lost Alhazen of Schröter.

CRISIUM, MARE. The Sea of Crises. A very conspicuous Mare, 280 miles by 350, enclosing an area of 66,000 square miles (larger than England). On it are three craterlets of some size (PICARD, PEIRCE and GRAHAM) and a multitude of craterlets, ridges and pits. Many mists have been recorded in the Mare, and the area between Picard and the jutting cape near Condorcet (CAPE AGARUM) is particularly subject to them.

DIONYSIUS. A bright crater 13 miles across, closely south of the Ariadæus Cleft. It appears very brilliant at full, as does a similar crater slightly north-east of it (CAYLEY). Thornton has found a dark band inside Dionysius, running to the north wall, but this requires a large aperture.

ENDYMION. A 78-mile walled plain near the limb, conspicuous under any lighting conditions on account of the darkness of its floor. Some of the patches inside it vary regularly each lunation.

EUDOXUS. A splendid 40-mile plain, with terraced walls rising to 11,000 feet. In many ways, Eudoxus is similar to its slightly larger companion, Aristoteles.

FIRMINICUS. A 35-mile crater south of the Mare Crisium, conspicuous because of its dark lunabase floor. Closely outside the north-east wall is a small lunabase 'lake'.

GODIN. A 27-mile crater with a central hill, in the highlands south of Ariadæus. Close by is a similar but rather larger crater, AGRIPPA.

GEMINUS. A conspicuous crater 55 miles across, near Cleomedes. It has terraced walls which rise to 12,000 feet above the sunken interior.

GAUSS. A high-walled formation over 100 miles across. Unfortunately, it is so close to the limb that it appears very foreshortened. Better placed, it would be a most imposing object.

HÆMUS MOUNTAINS. These mountains form the southern border of the Mare Serenitatis, and contain peaks rising to

8,000 feet. They end to the west in Cape Acherusia, and eastwards merge with the foothills of the Apennines.

HERCULES. The smaller companion of Atlas. Hercules is 45
miles across and 11,000 feet deep; the walls are deeply terraced,
and appear very brilliant at times, while the floor contains one
prominent crater and much fine detail.

HUMBOLDTIANUM, MARE (Humboldt's Sea). A small Mare
right on the limb, difficult to examine owing to its extreme foreshortening. Only Wilkins and Abineri have studied it in detail.
Were it better placed, it would probably appear very similar to
the Mare Crisium.

HYGINUS. A crater-depression about 4 miles across, associated with the famous crater-cleft. North of it is the area of
Hyginus N, suspected of change; and here too is an interesting
spiral mountain, the SCHNECKENBERG, which requires a high
power to be well seen. Some branches of the Hyginus cleft-
system join up with those from Ariadæus.

JULIUS CÆSAR. A low-walled, dark-floored formation not far
from Boscovitch, and rather similar to it, though considerably
larger.

LINNÉ. Situated on the Mare Serenitatis. Once a deep crater,
now, according to Thornton, a dome with a small deep central
pit.

MACROBIUS. A fine walled plain 42 miles across and 13,000
feet deep, near the Mare Crisium. There is a low, compound
central mountain mass.

MANILIUS. The chief crater of the Mare Vaporum. Manilius
is 25 miles in diameter, and has brilliant walls, so that it is
conspicuous under any conditions of lighting.

MARGINIS, MARE. The Marginal Sea. A small Mare west of
the Mare Crisium, so near the limb that it can never be well
seen.

MENELAUS. A brilliant crater in the Hæmus Mountains,
dazzlingly bright at full. It is 20 miles across and 6,000 feet
deep, with a central mountain.

METON. A compound enclosure west of Scoresby, not far
from the North Pole. It has low walls, and is over 100 miles long.

PLINIUS. A superb crater 'standing sentinel' on the strait
separating the Mare Serenitatis from the Mare Tranquillitatis.

Plinius is 30 miles across, with high terraced walls and a central structure.

POSIDONIUS. A walled plain 62 miles in diameter, with low, narrow walls, on the boundary between the Mare Serenitatis and the Lacus Somniorum. The floor contains much detail. Adjoining Posidonius to the west is a smaller, squarish formation, CHACORNAC, and west of Chacornac is a coastal crater, LE MONNIER, whose seaward wall has been broken down by the Mare lava, turning the formation into a bay.

PROCLUS. A brilliant crater east of the Mare Crisium, 18 miles in diameter and 8,000 feet deep. Proclus is one of the brightest points on the moon, and is the centre of a major ray-system. The rays from it cross the Mare Crisium, but not the Palus Somnii, which is bounded on either side by rays. In 1948, Thornton found dusky and bright streaks inside Proclus, since confirmed by Wilkins, D. C. Brown and other observers, including the writer.

SABINE. An 18-mile crater on the border of the Mare Tranquillitatis, almost on the equator. Thornton has found that it has a concentric inner wall. Closely north-east of Sabine is a crater of much the same size, RITTER, and north-east of Ritter are two small bright craters.

SCORESBY. A fine bright crater 36 miles across, with a twin-peaked central mountain. It lies near the North Pole, and is distinct under any illumination.

SHACKLETON. The North Polar crater. A large walled plain, only well seen under good conditions of libration. Its wall is broken in the south-east by a smaller but deeper crater, GIOJA, and to the north-west of Shackleton is a well-formed crater with a central peak, PEARY. West of Shackleton is a large compound enclosure, NANSEN.

SMYTHII, MARE. Smyth's Sea. A small plain on the equator, so close to the limb that it is exceedingly difficult to examine.

SOMNII, PALUS. The Marsh of Sleep. Really an extension of the Mare Tranquillitatis, bounded on the north-east and south-west by rays from Proclus. The colour is curious; it has been described variously as brownish, greenish and yellowish, and Barker considers that it is subject to variations.

SOMNIORUM, LACUS. The Lake of the Sleepers. A northward

extension of the Mare Serenitatis. It merges on the n⸍
with a smaller lake, LACUS MORTIS, the Lake of Deaᵗ

TARUNTIUS. An interesting crater south of Mar
38 miles in diameter, with very narrow walls and ϱ
hill. The floor contains a complete inner ring.

THALES. A 20-mile crater near the dark-floore
Thales is the centre of a ray-system; and betweer.
mion is a very old, battered formation known as

TRANQUILLITATIS, MARE. The Sea of Tranquilli′
major seas, but rather lacking in interesting deta
on to the Mare Serenitatis, Mare Vaporum, Mar
Mare Fœcunditatis.

TRIESNECKER. A bright 14-mile crater on ⁺ℎ.
close to the centre of the disk, interesting ᴐecause tℎ.
closely west of it is criss-crossed with clefts.

VITRUVIUS. A 20-mile crater not far fronᵣ Mount Argæus,
with bright walls and a dark floor. Some oᵣ ′he nearby mountains are so brilliant at times that Pickeriᴓ, believed them to
be snow-capped.

Second (north-east) quaₗ nt

The second quadrant consists maᴵ ′ᵤ of Mare-surface. In
addition to the great Mare Imbriuᴵᵗ there is a large part of
the Oceanus Procellarum, as well as r ᵣe than half of the Mare
Frigoris and a small portion of ⊸ᵢe Mare Nubium. Of the
craters, Copernicus, Aristarchus, Plato and Archimedes are
perhaps the most important, but it is safe to say that this
quadrant contains more than its fair share of interesting formations. The chief mountain ranges are the Carpathians, the
Juras, and the majestic, towering Apennines.

ÆSTUUM, SINUS. The Bay of Billows. A well-marked bay not
far from the centre of the disk, with a smooth and comparatively featureless surface. On its borders lie the great crater
Eratosthenes and the ruined Stadius.

ANAXAGORAS. A fine bright crater near the North Pole, 32
miles in diameter and 10,000 feet deep, with a splendid central
mountain. Anaxagoras is the centre of a prominent ray system,
and is thus distinct under any illumination.

APENNINES. The most impressive mountain range on the

over 600 miles long, with summits rising to 15,000 feet. st peak of all, MOUNT HUYGENS, has an altitude of 000 feet. The Apennines stretch from Mount Hadley) on the north to the noble crater Eratosthenes in nd form one part of the boundary of the Mare e foot-hills are extensive, and, on the Mare itself, fissures and clefts.

s. A 50-mile plain on the Mare Imbrium, with a ish-coloured floor overlaid with lunabase, and no entral mountain. The walls have been much re- to no more than 4,000 feet anywhere.

. On the Oceanus Procellarum; 29 miles in out 5,000 feet deep. The central peak is de- the bright est spot on the moon.

BEER. This, with its twin, FEUILLÉE, lies on the Mare Imbrium, between Archimedes and Timocharis. Each is about 8 miles in diameter. Beer and Feuillée seem to show optical variations in relative size each lunation, probably similar to those seen in Messier and Pickering.

CARPATHIAN MOUNTAINS. A rather broken range of mountains along the southern border of the Mare Imbrium. Altogether they extend for well over 100 miles, but there are no very high peaks–the loftiest is no more than 7,000 feet above the plain.

COPERNICUS. A superb crater, 56 miles from crest to crest, and the centre of the second most important ray-system on the moon.

ENCKE. A low-walled crater some 20 miles in diameter. It lies in the Oceanus Procellarum, south of Kepler.

ERATOSTHENES. A noble crater 38 miles across and over 16,000 feet deep, marking the termination of the Apennines. There is a lofty, complex central mountain, and the walls are deeply terraced.

EULER. A 19-mile crater, well placed on the Mare Imbrium, almost due west of Aristarchus.

FRIGORIS, MARE. The Sea of Cold. This extends into the first quadrant, and is one of the least important of the major seas. In general, it is ill-defined, with a colour described by some as dirty yellow (though the writer, slow to see colour of any kind on the moon, would describe it as dull grey). The most important crater on it is Archytas.

HARBINGER MOUNTAINS. A group of moderately lofty peaks north of Aristarchus. There are some clefts and domes in the area.

HARPALUS. A 22-mile crater north of the Sinus Iridum, which became famous when it was selected as the landing-ground for the first space-ship in the film *Destination Moon*. The walls rise to 16,000 feet above a comparatively featureless floor. There is no central mountain.

HELICON. A 13-mile crater, 5,000 feet deep, near the old destroyed seaward border of the Sinus Iridum. Closely west of it is a slightly smaller crater, LE VERRIER. Strangely enough, Helicon is distinct under any illumination, while Le Verrier virtually disappears under high light.

HERODOTUS. A darkish-floored crater, 23 miles in diameter and 4,000 feet deep, close to the brilliant Aristarchus. Herodotus is chiefly notable on account of the celebrated valley which starts from inside it.[1]

HEVEL. A walled plain almost on the equator, close to the limb; one of the Grimaldi group. Hevel is 70 miles in diameter, with low walls and central mountain. On the floor, which is noticeably convex, can be seen many delicate clefts. Closely east of Hevel is a larger and more broken walled plain, SVEN HEDIN.

IMBRIUM, MARE. The Sea of Showers. Undoubtedly the grandest and most perfect of all the lunar seas. It is more or less circular, with a diameter of some 700 miles. On it can be seen nearly all types of lunar formations. The main craters are Archimedes, Autolycus, Aristillus, Timocharis and Lambert. The area round Cassini and Aristillus is known as the PALUS NEBULARUM (the Marsh of Clouds) and the area between Archimedes and the Apennines as the PALUS PUTREDINIS (the Marsh of Decay). Except for the western strait, and the broad gap on the east where it merges with the Oceanus Procellarum, the Mare Imbrium is bordered by mountains (the Carpathians, Apennines, Caucasus, Alps and Juras).

IRIDUM, SINUS. The Bay of Rainbows. Probably the most

---

[1] There has been much discussion as to whether the valley starts right inside Herodotus, or outside the wall. The writer's 1952 observations with the 33-inch Meudon refractor indicate definitely that the former is the case.

beautiful object on the moon, particularly when it stands out from the blackness beyond the terminator. The seaward wall has been destroyed, and between the two capes of LAPLACE and HERACLIDES nothing remains apart from low, discontinuous ridges.

JURA MOUNTAINS. The mountains bordering Sinus Iridum, perhaps better termed 'mountainous highlands'.

KEPLER. A crater on the Oceanus Procellarum, 22 miles in diameter and 10,000 feet deep. There is a central mountain. Kepler is conspicuous under any lighting conditions, and is the centre of a major ray-system.

LAMBERT. An 18-mile crater on the Mare Imbrium, conspicuous on account of its isolated position. To the south is a smaller crater, PYTHEAS, and to the north-east a bright isolated mountain, LA HIRE.

LANDSBERG. A fine bright crater, 28 miles in diameter and almost 10,000 feet deep, exactly on the lunar equator, southeast of Copernicus.

LICHTENBERG. A small crater between Aristarchus and the limb, surrounded by a light nimbus. Mädler often recorded a reddish tint nearby, seen in recent years by Barcroft, Haas and Baum.

MEDII, SINUS. The Central Bay. So called because it includes the centre of the visible disk. The chief crater on it is Triesnecker.

OLBERS. A large crater near the equator and very close to the limb, 40 miles in diameter and 10,000 feet deep. It is very conspicuous, and is the centre of a major ray-system.

PHILOLAUS. This and its companion, ANAXIMANDER, lie near the northern limb, west of Pythagoras. Philolaus is 46 miles in diameter, and has a terraced wall rising to 12,000 feet. A reddish tint has been seen in it from time to time, and even the writer has recorded a very faint purplish-brown hue!

PICO. A splendid 8,000-foot mountain on the Mare Imbrium, south of Plato. It should be better described as a mountain mass, as there are at least three major peaks. Some way southeast is a slightly less lofty mountain, PITON, which has a summit craterlet only visible in large telescopes. Between Pico and Piton is a bright little crater, PIAZZI SMYTH.

PROCELLARUM, OCEANUS. The Ocean of Storms. This is the largest of all the 'seas'. It has an area of 2 million square miles (much larger than European Russia, and nearly twice the size of the Mediterranean), but is not well-defined, and connects with the Mare Imbrium, the Mare Frigoris (by way of the Sinus Roris), and the Mare Nubium. It extends into the third quadrant.

PLATO. The celebrated 'Greater Black Lake' of Hevelius. It is 60 miles across, with walls less than 4,000 feet in height, but is very conspicuous under any illumination. The dark, steely floor shows strange variations which can only be due to local obscurations. Abutting on Plato to the south is a 'ghost' ring of similar size, and this Schröter named 'Newton'; but Beer and Mädler, feeling that the formation was too obscure for the world's greatest scientist, transferred the name to a deep formation near the South Pole, and relegated the 'ghost' to anonymity.

PYTHAGORAS. A splendid walled plain 85 miles in diameter; it is one of a number of magnificent formations along the north-east limb which would be most imposing were they better placed. Others are XENOPHANES (to the south of Pythagoras) and THORNTON (to the north). The latter is quite invisible at mean libration, though its smaller companion, ARTHUR, can be seen.

RORIS, SINUS. The Bay of Dews. A rather ill-defined lunabase area connecting the Oceanus Procellarum with the Mare Frigoris.

STADIUS. The famous 'ghost' on the border of the Sinus Æstuum.

STRAIGHT RANGE. A peculiar range of mountains in the Mare Imbrium, east of Plato. The length is only 40 miles, and the height under 6,000 feet; but the range is conspicuous as it begins and ends abruptly, and is curiously regular in form.

SPITZBERGEN MOUNTAINS. A clump of bright little hills on the Mare Imbrium, some way north of Archimedes.

TIMOCHARIS. A 23-mile crater on the Mare Imbrium, 7,000 feet deep, and conspicuous on account of its comparative isolation. It is the centre of a ray-system, but the rays are so similar in colour to the Mare surface that they are not easy to detect. Mists in Timocharis have been recorded by Barcroft and others.

Third (south-east) quadrant

The third quadrant contains many interesting features. The northern portion is occupied largely by seas; the southern part of the Oceanus Procellarum, nearly all the Mare Nubium, and the comparatively small Mare Humorum. The southern part is rugged upland, and here we find some of the largest walled plains on the moon, including Clavius, Bailly (the largest of all), Schickard and Newton Also in this quadrant are Tycho, the ray-crater, and the celebrated plateau Wargentin; the series of great walled plains of which Ptolemæus is the most important member; and the dark-floored Grimaldi and Riccioli, as well as the Straight Wall. The only mountain ranges well placed on the disk, the Riphæns and the Percy Mountains, are comparatively low, but along the limb run the Dörfel and Rook ranges, which are among the highest on the entire moon.

ALPETRAGIUS. A conspicuous crater not far from the central meridian, close to Alphons. It is 27 miles in diameter, and 12,000 feet deep. There is an unusually massive central peak, and on its summit Dr. Wilkins, at Meudon, discovered a minute craterlet–immediately confirmed by the present writer, using the same instrument.

ALPHONS. A great walled plain 70 miles across, with rather broken walls rising to a maximum of 7,000 feet. The floor contains a reduced central mountain, and some dark patches which seem to show periodical variations each lunation. Alphons is a member of the Ptolemæus group of walled plains.

ARZACHEL. Another large walled plain, adjoining Alphons to the south. It is smaller but deeper than Alphons (60 miles in diameter, 13,000 feet deep), and has a central mountain rising 5,000 feet above the floor.

BAILLY. This, the largest of all the walled plains, is 183 miles in diameter and 14,000 feet deep. The floor contains a mass of detail, including one large crater, HARE. It is a pity that Bailly is so badly placed, as it would otherwise be a most imposing object. It lies very close to the limb, not a great distance from the South Pole.

BILLY. A crater 30 miles in diameter and 4,000 feet deep, on the borders of the Oceanus Procellarum, not far from Grimaldi.

Its dark, iron-grey floor makes it distinct under any illumination. Nearby is a normal-hued crater of similar size, HANSTEEN.

BIRT. An 11-mile, fairly deep crater close to the Straight Wall, containing two dark radial bands visible with moderate telescopes. Outside, to the east, is a fine cleft, with crater-like enlargements.

BULLIALDUS. A magnificent crater on the Mare Nubium, 39 miles in diameter, and with fine terraced walls rising some 8,000 feet above an interior which contains a prominent central mountain.

CLAVIUS. A splendid walled plain in the far south, often stated to be the largest formation of its kind—though actually it must yield this title to Bailly. Clavius is 145 miles across, with walls rising to 17,000 feet above the deeply depressed interior. The walls are broken by two large craters, RUTHERFURD (south wall) and PORTER (north wall), and a line of craters extends across the floor, which also contains a large amount of finer detail.

CRUGER. A low-walled crater 30 miles across, not far from the limb, south of Grimaldi. Like Billy, it has a dark floor which makes it easily recognizable at any time.

DARWIN. A large walled plain some 70 miles in diameter, closely south of Crüger. Its walls are very broken, and it is not at all conspicuous, but it is interesting, as it contains the large dome to which attention was first drawn by Barker.

DOPPELMAYER Formerly an important crater, now no more than a bay on the borders of the Mare Humorum—though the seaward wall can still be traced, and there are the remains of a central mountain. It is 40 miles in diameter.

DORFEL MOUNTAINS. A lofty range of mountains right on the limb, and consequently never well seen. Some peaks rise to almost 30,000 feet, and are probably the highest on the moon apart from the Leibnitz.

EUCLIDES. A crater 7 miles in diameter and 2,000 feet deep, close to the Riphæn Mountains. It is remarkable for being surrounded by an extensive, triangular bright nimbus—the largest of its kind on the moon.

FRA MAURO. A walled plain 50 miles across, on the Mare Nubium. Its walls have been so reduced that they are now discontinuous. Two similarly dilapidated rings, BONPLAND and PARRY, adjoin it to the south, and further south still is another similar formation, GUERIKÉ.

GASSENDI One of the finest walled plains on the moon. It lies on the border of the Mare Humorum, and is 55 miles across. Although the walls have been damaged by the Mare lava, one peak rises to 9,000 feet. On the floor there is a central mountain, as well as several craters and hills and an interesting system of clefts.

GRIMALDI. Close to the equator, and close to the limb. Grimaldi is 120 miles across, with very low, broken walls, and an iron-grey floor. Generally this floor is the darkest spot on the moon, and certain areas of it are probably variable.

HEINSIUS. A strange formation 45 miles across, broken in the south-east by two large craters. It lies some way east of Tycho.

HESIODUS. A crater 28 miles in diameter, close to Pitatus, on the southern border of the Mare Nubium. It is associated with a large cleft, which runs eastwards from it, and can be seen with a very small telescope.

HIPPALUS. Another bay on the edge of the Mare Humorum, similar in many ways to Döppelmayer. The seaward wall has been almost levelled, but the central peak still exists, though it is much reduced. There are many clefts in the region west of Hippalus.

HUMORUM, MARE. The Sea of Moisture. A small Mare connected with the Oceanus Procellarum. The old upland between the two 'seas' can still be traced here and there. The floor contains no major formation, but there are many hills and pits. The Mare is bordered on the east by an upland region known as the PERCY MOUNTAINS.

KIES. A 25-mile crater close to Bullialdus. The walls have been very badly damaged by lava, and now rise to only 2,000 feet. South of Kies is a smaller crater, Kies A, which contains a dark radial band discovered by Abineri in 1948.

LETRONNE. A large crater 70 miles across, on the border of the Oceanus Procellarum. Lava has destroyed the seaward wall, turning Letronne into a bay. The old central mountain can still be seen.

MAGINUS. A partly ruined walled plain near Tycho, over 100

miles in diameter. The walls are lofty but irregular, rising in one or two places to 14,000 feet. Maginus is curiously obscure under high light, although it is not true to say (as some have done) that it totally disappears at full moon.

MERCATOR. A 28-mile crater, 5,000 feet deep, on the border of the Mare Nubium, south of Bullialdus. The only marked difference between Mercator and its companion, CAMPANUS, is that Mercator has a darker floor.

MERSENIUS. A prominent crater near Gassendi, 45 miles across and 7,000 feet deep. The floor is decidedly convex. There are many clefts nearby.

MOORE. A small crater 12 miles across, east of Bullialdus. It interrupts a prominent cleft. There are two dark radial bands running to the inner east wall.

MORËTUS. A splendid walled plain 75 miles in diameter, with terraced walls rising to 15,000 feet above a floor which contains a lofty central mountain. Unfortunately, Morètus is so close to the South Pole that it can never be seen to advantage.

NEWTON. A vast compound formation close to Morètus. The walls rise to a maximum of 29,000 feet, so that Newton is the deepest crater on the moon. It can never be well seen, owing to its bad position.

NUBIUM, MARE. The Sea of Clouds. This is one of the largest of all the seas, and contains many interesting objects The chief walled formations are Bullialdus and the Fra Mauro - Gueriké group.

PITATUS. A crater 50 miles in diameter, on the southern border of the Mare Nubium Its seaward wall has been badly damaged, and the floor overlaid with lunabase, though the central peak can still be seen. Dr. Wilkins has justly likened it to a huge lagoon.

PTOLEMÆUS. A 90-mile walled plain close to the apparent centre of the disk. The walls are broken, and of no great height; the floor contains a large craterlet, LYOT, and many pits and shallow, saucer-like depressions. Dr. Wilkins has used a superb photograph taken at the Pic du Midi to construct an elaborate chart, so that Ptolemæus is probably the best-mapped formation on the moon.

PURBACH. A large walled plain, 75 miles across, with walls

rising to 8,000 feet. It is the northern member of a chain of three great formations south of the Ptolemæus chain.

REGIOMONTANUS. A distorted walled plain between Purbach and Walter, 80 miles by 65 miles. The walls are broken, and there is a low central elevation.

RICCIOLI. The smaller companion of Grimaldi. Riccioli is 100 miles long, with low, broken walls. The northern area of the floor is almost as dark as the interior of Grimaldi. In a small telescope it appears almost smooth, but high powers reveal much detail.

RIPHÆN MOUNTAINS. A low range on the Mare Nubium, rising to no more than 3,000 feet. The peaks seem to have suffered from some kind of erosion.

ROOK MOUNTAINS. A very lofty limb-range, continued north-wards by the CORDILLERAS. The highest Rook peaks surpass 20,000 feet.

SCHEINER. A magnificent 70-mile crater, with terraced walls rising to 18,000 feet. It would appear much more imposing but for the fact that it is very close to Clavius. Near Scheiner is a similar but slightly smaller formation, BLANCANUS.

SCHICKARD. A most interesting walled plain, near the limb. It is 134 miles in diameter, with walls which are lofty in places—one peak rises to 9,000 feet—but very irregular in height. The floor abounds in detail. Mists have been seen from time to time inside Schickard.

SIRSALIS. A 20-mile crater south of Grimaldi. It has broken into its 'twin', the slightly larger but rather shallower formation BERTAUD. It is associated with a great cleft, visible in very small telescopes.

STRAIGHT WALL. The celebrated fault in the Mare Nubium.

SCHILLER. A most peculiarly shaped formation between Clavius and Schickard, 112 miles long, but only 60 wide. Actually, Schiller is the result of the coalescence of two ringed plains; the dividing wall can still be traced under suitable conditions.

THEBIT. A 37-mile crater close to Arzachel, with high ter-raced walls. It is broken in the north-east by a smaller crater, Thebit A, which is in turn broken by a small craterlet with a central hill.

TYCHO. The celebrated ray-crater; 54 miles in diameter, with high terraced walls, distinct under any conditions of illumination.

VITELLO. A strange formation on the border of the Mare Humorum. It is 30 miles in diameter, and some 4,500 feet deep; inside it is a complete ring, not quite concentric with the outer wall. There is a central hill, upon which is a summit craterlet only visible with large telescopes.

WALTER. The third of the great walled plains of the Purbach group. Walter is 90 miles in diameter, with a high, massive wall. Adjoining it to the east is a vast ruined plain, HORBIGER.

WARGENTIN. The famous plateau, close to Schickard. There are no other plateaux on the moon comparable to it in size, and it is most unfortunate that it lies so close to the limb. In 1952 Dr. Wilkins and the writer, at Meudon, charted over fifty objects on the 'floor', but with ordinary telescopes little can be seen apart from a long axial ridge.

Fourth (south-west) quadrant

This quadrant is occupied mainly by the rugged southern uplands, and abounds in detail. The only sea-areas are the Mare Nectaris and most of the Mare Fœcunditatis; the only ranges, the badly placed Leibnitz and the much less lofty Altai Mountains. Clefts are comparatively rare. There are, however, many large and important walled formations, notably Theophilus, Stöfler, Langrenus, Petavius, Vendelinus, Furnerius and Albategnius.

ALBATEGNIUS. A tremendous walled plain closely west of Ptolemæus, near the apparent centre of the disk. It is 80 miles across, with broad terraced walls of rather uneven altitude, rising at one point to 15,000 feet above the rather dark floor. There is no central mountain. The south-east wall is disturbed by KLEIN, a deep crater 20 miles in diameter, with central hill.

ALTAI MOUNTAINS. The most important upland mountain range, but perhaps better described as a line of faults, as they are precipitous on the west (up to 6,000 feet on an average, with higher crests, one of which attains 13,000 feet); but on the east the ground slopes gently down to a broad plain. The range is rather more than 300 miles long, and is roughly concentric with the south-eastern border of the Mare Nectaris.

AUSTRALE, MARE. The Southern Sea. Not properly a 'sea' at all, but a mere surface deposit of lunabase. It lies close to the limb, and is best identified by a large, dark-floored crater, OKEN, nearby.

CAPELLA. A 30-mile crater, not far from Theophilus. It has an exceptionally massive central mountain, on the top of which is a minute craterlet.

CATHARINA. The southernmost member of the Theophilus group. Catharina is 70 miles in diameter, with walls that have been considerably damaged in places. The floor is very rough, though there is no central elevation. Catharina and its neighbour, Cyrillus, are connected by a broad valley.

CUVIER. A 50-mile crater in the highlands west of Tycho, 12,000 feet deep. It is close to a shallower, larger and less regular formation, HERACLITUS; and there are many other ringplains in this area very similar to Cuvier.

CYRILLUS. Between Catharina and Theophilus, on the border of the Mare Nectaris. Cyrillus is 65 miles in diameter, and its north wall has been badly damaged by the intrusion of Theophilus. There is a reduced group of elevations not far from the centre, and much other floor detail.

FABRITIUS. A fairly deep walled plain 55 miles in diameter, between Mare Australe and the Altai range. Closely south-west of it is a slightly smaller but rather deeper formation, METIUS, and adjoining Fabritius to the south is the vast ruin JANSSEN.

FŒCUNDITATIS, MARE. The Sea of Fertility. One of the larger seas of the western hemisphere; its area is 160,000 square miles, so that it is considerably larger than Poland. It is less well defined than some of the great Maria, however, and the only notable objects on it are Messier and Taruntius, though three tremendous formations, Langrenus, Vendelinus and Petavius, lie along its western border.

FRACASTORIUS. A 60-mile bay on the Mare Nectaris. The south wall is still lofty, but of the old north wall only a few hummocks remain. The badly battered central mountain can still be traced, though the whole floor is overlaid with lunabase.

FURNERIUS. The southern member of the great Western Chain

of walled plains. Furnerius is 80 miles in diameter, with terraced walls rising to more than 11,000 feet above a floor which contains much delicate detail. There is no central mountain.

GUTENBERG. This and its companion, GOCLENIUS, lie on the highland between the Mare Fœcunditatis and the Mare Nectaris. Gutenberg is a 45-mile, low-walled formation of rather distorted shape; Goclenius smaller, deeper and more regular. To the north lie some delicate clefts.

HIPPARCHUS. A noble ruin close to the centre of the apparent disk. It is 84 miles across, but the walls have been so ruined that they are now discontinuous, and nowhere rise to more than 4,000 feet. The floor contains one large crater, HORROCKS, and much lesser detail. Between Hipparchus and its smaller but better-preserved companion Albategnius are two prominent formations, HIND and HALLEY.

JANSSEN. The great ruined formation south of Fabritius.

LANGRENUS. A splendid crater near the equator, on the borders of the Mare Fœcunditatis. It is 85 miles in diameter, with a wall reaching 9,000 feet; and there is a high central mountain.

MADLER. A 20-mile crater on the strait separating the Mare Nectaris from the Mare Tranquillitatis, only notable because it lies on the border of a much larger ghost ring.

MAUROLYCUS. A walled plain in the southern uplands, 75 miles across. Its walls rise to some 14,000 feet.

MESSIER. This and its companion, PICKERING, lie in the Mare Fœcunditatis, near the equator. They can be identified under any conditions of illumination because of the curious 'comet' double ray extending eastwards from Pickering.

NECTARIS, MARE. The Sea of Nectar. A great 'bay' of the Mare Tranquillitatis, though probably a separate subsidence product. The darkish floor contains one conspicuous craterlet (ROSSE) and some clefts and ridges, mainly concentric with the coasts and perhaps analogous to the terraces of smaller walled formations.

PALITZSCH. A formation closely west of Petavius. It is often described as one of the few genuinely 'irregular' formations, as it is 60 miles long and only 20 broad, and at first sight resembles a huge walled gorge, but in October 1952 the writer, observing at Cambridge University with the 25-inch Newall refractor, saw that it is really a crater-chain, made up of several rings whose separating walls have been largely destroyed.

PETAVIUS. A splendid crater on the borders of the Mare Fœcunditatis. It is 100 miles in diameter, with peaks in its rampart rising to 11,000 feet. The floor contains a lofty central mountain group, from which a rugged cleft runs to the south-east wall; and there is much other interior detail.

PICCOLOMINI. A 56-mile crater some way south of Fracastorius, marking the termination of the Altai range. There is a central mountain, and the highest peaks of the rampart rise to 15,000 feet above the floor.

RHEITA. A crater 42 miles across, connected with a great valley 115 miles long and 15 wide. This valley is probably made up of confluent craterlets. Some way north of it is a shallower valley, near the craters REICHENBACH and STEAVENSON.

SCOTT. A walled plain 66 miles in diameter, very close to the limb and not far from the South Pole. It is joined on the south by an equally large but rather shallower crater, AMUNDSEN, not visible at all under conditions of mean libration; and further west, along the limb, is another large formation, DEMONAX.

STEINHEIL. This and its companion, WATT, lie closely south-west of Janssen. Steinheil, the smaller and deeper, is 42 miles in diameter, and has intruded on to Watt's floor.

STOFLER. A tremendous, darkish-floored plain in the southern uplands, 90 miles across. Its south-west wall is broken by the intrusion of a large crater, FARADAY. Stöfler's floor appears smooth and lake-like under low illumination, but actually contains much detail.

THEOPHILUS. Theophilus rivals Copernicus for the title of "Monarch of the Moon". It is a superb crater on the borders of the Mare Nectaris, 65 miles across, with terraced walls rising to 18,000 feet above the sunken floor. There is a lofty, complex central mountain group; Pickering believed some of the summits to be snow-covered! To the south, Theophilus has broken into its older neighbour, Cyrillus.

VENDELINUS. One of the great Western Chain. Vendelinus, which lies between Langrenus and Petavius, has been more distorted than its neighbours; the walls are comparatively low, and broken to the north-west by a large crater, SMITH. There is no central mountain, but the floor contains a vast amount of detail. Vendelinus is 100 miles in diameter.

VLACQ. One of a group of ring-plains near Janssen, the other members of the group being ROSENBERGER, HOMMEL, NEARCH, PITISCUS, BIELA, and the peculiar, heart-shaped HAGECIUS. Vlacq is 56 miles in diameter and 10,000 feet deep, with a central mountain.

VOGEL. A peculiar formation near Albategnius. It is made up of three confluent craters, and should therefore be properly classed as a crater-chain.

WERNER. A 45-mile, 15,000-foot crater near Walter, with a central mountain. The light spot at the foor of the inner north-east wall seems to have faded during the last 100 years, as Beer and Mädler said that it was as brilliant as Aristarchus–which is not the case now, though it is still bright. Closely south-west of Werner is a similar formation, ALIACENSIS, slightly larger but not so deep; and in the area enclosed by Theophilus, Aliacensis and Albategnius are three more pairs of twins–APIAN and PLAYFAIR, AZOPHI and ABENEZRA, and ABULFEDA and ALMANON.

WILHELM HUMBOLDT. A walled plain 120 miles across and 16,000 feet deep. Were it better placed it would rank with Clavius and Ptolemæus; but it is right on the limb, near Petavius, and consequently never well seen. There is a good deal of detail on the floor. Between Wilhelm Humboldt and Palitzsch is a large walled plain, PHILLIPS.

ZAGUT. A 50-mile crater in the southern uplands, not far from Maurolycus. It is one of a group of five, the remaining members being RABBI LEVI, CELSIUS, LINDENAU and WILKINS.

INDEX TO FORMATIONS REFERRED
TO IN THE TEXT

220

GENERAL INDEX

CPSIA information can be obtained
at www.ICGtesting.com
Printed in the USA
FSOW02n2106120815
9895FS